WITHDRAWN

MIDNIGHT IN THE CITY

IN THE

CITY

a rEporteR's joUrney
to AmeriCa's darK plaCes
rOcks his viEw of
reIIGIoN

HaL dOnAIdSON
WITH kIrK nOoNan

Midnight in the City
*A reporter's journey to America's dark places
rocks his view of the church*
By Hal Donaldson with Kirk Noonan

Printed in the United States of America
ISBN: 1-880689-14-6
Copyright 2005, Onward Books, Inc.

Cover design by Matt Key

Scripture quotations are taken from the *New International Version*, Copyright 1973, 1978, 1984, International Bible Society.

deDicATiOn

Dedicated to my children—Lindsay, Erin-Rae, Lauren and Haly. May they know what it means to serve Jesus by serving others.

AutHor's nOte

Many of the descriptions in this book are graphic and disturbing, which some readers may find offensive. Some details and dialog have been toned down, but the authors and publisher believed it was important for this book to be an honest portrayal of the despair and depravity in America's cities. Some of the descriptions, sequences and events have been altered for dramatic effect and to protect the identity of the persons featured in this book. Many names have also been changed because conversations were recorded without the participants' knowledge.

Because of the graphic nature of this account, some parents may choose to read the book along with their younger teenagers. Youth groups, Sunday School classes and small groups may also choose to read it simultaneously and then reflect on the discussion questions at the end of the book.

Midnight in the City is not intended to be a criticism of government, social agencies, churches or civic groups. In recent years, the cities featured in this book have made great strides to improve the conditions and quality of life of their citizens. One thing hasn't changed, however: people everywhere are still desperate for hope.

contents

Special thanks to Dick Vass, Matt and Sherry McPherson, Bob and Rosa Clay, Ken and Peggy Horn, Matt Key, Joel Kilpatrick, Mike Ennis, Marc Whitmore, Shirley Speer, Steve Wilson, Ken Dobson, Danette McCabe, Spencer Jones, Bob Mathieu, Jesse Miranda, Scott Temple, Randy Hurst, Gerry Hindy, David Cribbs, Mike Messner, Brad Trask, Mike McClaflin, Barry Corey and Scott Wynant.

I was 12 years old the day I found my father praying alone
in our church's tiny sanctuary. As the pastor, he was kneeling
at the altar calling out to God for our family, church and
community. Not wanting to disturb him, I listened quietly
from the front pew. As my ears soaked in his warm prayers,
my eyes scanned his body and rested on the soles of his
shoes. There, I spied large holes exposing his socks.

Suddenly, an anger I had never known ripped through me.
It was as if I had been awakened to a horrible reality: we
were poor. For so long, I had refused to believe it, but now
everything was clear. I was sick of living in a room in our
church and I was tired of seeing my mom and dad always
giving to others, but never receiving anything in return.

Rather than brood over our plight or wallow in self-pity, I
vowed to do something about it. Someday I would earn all
the money our family needed, I said. Never again would my
parents have to struggle to put food on the table.

But little did I know that our family's financial situation
was going to get even worse. A short time later, my dad
was hit and killed by a drunken driver and my mother was
seriously injured. Instantly we became children of a disabled
widow, surviving on food stamps and handouts. I was the
oldest of four children, so when the social workers came to
our house they interrogated me to make sure we were still
deserving of special assistance.

As I entered my teenage years, there were times the soles
on my shoes wore so thin my socks were exposed—just like

my dad's. Our cupboards were often bare and buying new clothes wasn't an option. But such struggles only served to strengthen my resolve never to be poor.

Eventually life got easier as my mother climbed the ladder from part-time mail clerk to purchasing agent in her company. And, I was also able to find work after school, doing everything I could to keep the bill collectors off our backs.

By my mid-20s I was well on my way to the life I coveted. I felt good about my writing career and was satisfied with my relationship with Christ. I went to church on Sundays, paid my tithes, and even gave money to people in need. Where my dad worked among people in the trenches, I was content to live out my faith in suburbia by occasionally writing crisp, clean checks for worthy church projects.

But, in time, I realized my lifestyle lacked purpose and fulfillment. Self-centeredness was creeping into my heart and my religion had become powerless and ritualistic. Although I didn't stray from my moral moorings, it was obvious I had lost my way. The quest for financial freedom had left me empty.

As I examined my soul and asked God for answers, He revealed that I had forsaken my roots. Unlike my father, I had isolated myself from the poor and become ignorant of their plight. Rather than investing in a relationship with God, I had thrown everything into being religious. Instead of praying and believing that God could transform our nation's cities, I had simply mailed in a few donations to ease my conscience. Denominationalism and apathy had replaced genuine love, compassion and concern for others. In worldly terms I was everything I ever wanted to be, but in spiritual terms I was living without a divine purpose.

While on a writing assignment I checked into an upscale hotel. In my room that night—surrounded by luxury—I broke down and cried about what my life had become. I realized that for years I had overestimated the importance of my profession and possessions and their usefulness to God while totally underestimating the power of sacrifice, obedience and the guidance of the Holy Spirit. I knew I had to break out of the religious bubble and get a fresh start. I had to do something radical.

That's when I felt impressed to write a series of magazine articles on life in the inner city. I set out to walk the streets of eight major cities at night and to ride with the police on the midnight shift. This, I hoped, would also reconnect my heart to the poverty and despair of so many men, women and children.

What I found in these cities was disturbing, yet life-changing. With the mind-set of a journalist—rather than a minister—I ventured into a brothel, a homeless shelter, a jail cell, a homosexual nightclub, and more. I helped police chase down thieves and participated in stakeouts. I descended into many of America's dark places, often putting myself at risk. But it was there that I rediscovered the heart of Jesus for the suffering and deceived; it was there that I found my way.

The persons I interviewed and the experiences I had resembled scenes from a Hollywood movie. Each was so unique and sometimes so outlandish that my senses were shaken and my soul was stirred. Some of the experiences were not recorded in this book because they were too graphic and offensive. But each encounter served to change my heart and attitude toward those who are hurting or locked into lifestyles controlled by sin.

I did the reporting for this book and a series of magazine articles some years ago, before God transformed my life and launched Convoy of Hope, a ministry to the poor in the United States and around the world. Only recently did I feel the liberty to share the details of this deeply personal spiritual journey. I feared the reaction from church leaders to such an honest, unsanitized chronicle of life in America's inner cities. And I was hesitant to expose the fact that some churches and believers have lost their compassion for the poor and forsaken—and have lost sight of their mission.

But, my concerns began to fade when the pastor of an effective, multi-cultural church challenged me to publish the book. "The story must be told; Christians need to know the truth about what's happening in the nation and the church," he said. With his encouragement, the Lord's prodding, and the counsel of various inner-city leaders, I concluded the message of this book could not be pent up any longer. Now was the time for people like you to read *Midnight in the City*. It's my prayer that it will change your life as the journey changed mine.

—Hal Donaldson

"Suppose a brother or sister is without clothes and daily food. If one of you says to him, 'Go, I wish you well; keep warm and well fed,' but does nothing about his physical needs, what good is it?"

—*James 2:16*

ChaPter oNe

Naked in the City

The police sergeant sat in his windowless office in the precinct's station and clipped the end of a fresh cigar. Piles of rap sheets, reports and photos of perpetrators competed for space on his desk. Hanging crooked on the smoke-stained wall directly behind him were "most wanted" posters. Two banged up file cabinets and a leaning coat rack consumed two corners.

He lit up, took a long drag on the cheap cigar, exhaled, then measured me from behind the smoke. His hollow eyes told me he was disappointed at my youth. Like most people he probably thought I was younger than my 34 years. I shifted in my seat and waited for him to speak. Instead, he rolled the cigar between his thick fingers and took another drag. After what seemed like minutes of him sizing me up, he kicked his heels atop the desk and the mood changed.

"What's your name?"

"Hal," I said, intimidated.

He let my name hang in the air like foul-smelling cigar smoke. *Maybe this was a bad idea*, I thought. *Maybe I should have started in a smaller city.*

Too late; I was here. More than that I was determined to

see where this adventure would take me. With that settled, I mustered the nerve to ask a question.

"And yours?"

"Sarge."

My eyes searched his desk for a nameplate, but could find none.

"You ever done a cop ride-along before?" he asked, not waiting for an answer. "This is New York and you're riding on the night shift."

I swallowed hard. "That's what I'm here for."

The sergeant jumped to his feet. He was imposingly tall and built like a linebacker. His face was chiseled, but worn. Evidently, the cigars, late nights at the bars and the endless game of chasing bad guys had taken their toll.

"Follow me," he grumbled between clenched teeth that held the cigar in place.

I followed him into the hallway where he introduced me to a burly and equally brusque officer. We shook hands and made small talk. My companion for the evening was a veteran of the force, unimpressed that a reporter would be tagging along with him and, I guessed, unfazed by most anything we might see on the streets.

With a bulletproof vest hugging my chest, we began cruising the streets. It didn't take long for the night of action to begin. Over the radio we received orders to investigate a missing person complaint. Within minutes we pulled into "the projects"—a row of low rent, high-rise apartments. By the fierce stares of its residents I knew my blonde hair was the wrong calling card. Undeterred, I shadowed the officer up three flights of stairs to apartment 313. The stench emanating from the apartment led us to believe there might be a dead body inside. The officer's knuckles pounded the door.

"Police!" he shouted.

No answer.

He pounded some more.

"Police! Open up."

Still no answer.

"Let's find the manager or someone who has a key," he barked in frustration.

When the manager couldn't locate a key, the officer warned, "We're gonna have to break the door down."

I'd seen doors knocked down on television a hundred times and it always looked easy. The officer kicked the door several times. Though he was powerfully built and wearing combat-style boots, the door didn't budge.

"Dead-bolted piece of [expletive]," he said.

"Do you want me to ask the neighbors if they've seen anything?" I interrupted.

Instead of answering, he gave the door one more kick. Nothing.

"Yeah, maybe someone knows something."

He knocked on the door across the hall, which opened cautiously after a minute or two. Through the small crack I could see a sliver of poverty: bare, uncarpeted floor; furniture that looked like it had been pulled from the trash, broken tables and splintered bookcases sitting in the middle of the room. Two children wandered around listlessly. One kid, no more than a year and a half old, had urine dripping out of her soiled diaper and down her leg.

"Yeah?" said the frightened mother.

"Lookin' for the guy in 313," the officer said.

"Haven't seen him—try over there," she said.

We proceeded down the hall and banged on another door. The man who answered was nearly incoherent, one eye closed, the other unable to look straight. The apartment behind him was dark and filled with cigarette smoke, and smelled like human excrement. From an unseen television I heard the disgusting grunts of a pornographic movie.

"What? Hey," the guy said, rubbing his face.

"You seen the fella in 313?" the officer asked, holding his breath.

"Huh? No, I don't know whose [expletive] lives there," he said, reaching for a lighter in his robe pocket and flicking the flame absent-mindedly.

We marched upstairs and knocked on three more doors before giving up on the neighbors.

"Let's try the fire escape," the officer said as though I were his partner. "We'll go through the window."

We climbed the rest of the stairs to the roof where the officer held me back with a wave of his hand. He opened the door quickly and stepped out with his hand on his gun. He made sure the place was clear, and then motioned me onto the roof.

"Roofs are a common place for drug deals to go down," he said. "You don't just come waltzing out on roofs."

As we tiptoed over the gravel I noticed a few hypodermic needles and cigarette lighters. We scurried to the building's edge and climbed down the fire escape. When we reached the third floor the officer smashed the window of the apartment with his flashlight and opened the pane. I stooped down behind him and stepped into an apartment shin-deep in trash: jugs, food boxes and wrappers, filthy clothes, dozens of pornographic magazines, sleazy videos, balled-up sheets, beer cans, whiskey bottles and toilet paper.

I didn't know which way to turn, but the officer trudged to the other side of the room. There, under a thin sheet, was a man—alive or dead, I couldn't tell. The officer pulled back the sheet with his flashlight and the form moved. He was naked, unshaven, and in a drunken stupor.

The officer promptly radioed for another vehicle to transport the man to a detoxification facility.

"Hey," the officer said to me, "help me pick him up."

I began to obey, but my mind, body and soul hesitated. The smell in the apartment was nauseating: thick, unavoidable, like warm death and sewage, and it seemed to emanate from the man on the bed. I felt like I was going to vomit. I didn't budge.

"Hurry up," he said, irritated.

Finally, feeling the scorn of the officer, I cautiously stepped through the piles of debris and grabbed one of the man's arms. He couldn't even lift himself. We put a reeking bathrobe and a pair of pants on him, and then draped his floppy arms around our necks so we could lug him downstairs.

With each step down the cement stairs, my shame grew. I could almost hear God's disgust and feel His disappointment: Who do you think you are? Do you really think you're too good to get your hands dirty? After all I've done for you—you won't even extend a hand to help this man?

As the detox vehicle pulled away, I climbed into the squad car and waited for the officer to return. I stared absently at the dashboard, disappointed in myself and pondering how far I had drifted from the image of Christ. I silently asked, *Was this trip to New York really about discovering the plight of people in need so I could write a few magazine articles or was I hoping somehow to reignite my faith that had grown into a Sunday morning ritual?*

The truth erupted in my mind: I was weary of my brand of religion, where I showcased my successes and buried my failures on Sundays. There wasn't space in my church life for confession or human frailty. Somehow, on Sundays, worshipping Christ and learning God's Word had been demoted to a secondary concern. Church had become primarily about networking with friends, maintaining my image and meeting the expectations of others. I had begun to take my church for granted—not soaking in all it had to offer or stretching myself to support its various ministries. To everyone but me, I was a model Christian. I obeyed the Ten Commandments and even performed acts of kindness every now and then, but there was something religious and prideful residing in my heart that prevented me from fully walking in the footsteps of Christ. Somewhere along the way, I had stopped growing in my knowledge of Jesus. And emulating Him was no longer my highest priority.

Why couldn't I feel safe being real at church? I asked myself. Was I afraid of the criticism that fellow churchgoers would heap on me if they knew how powerless and empty I felt inside—especially on Sundays. Would they understand?

As of late, seldom did I enter church anticipating God's presence. His presence was there, but my heart wasn't prepared to receive what He had for me. Church had become a place where I didn't feel comfortable being transparent with God and being vulnerable to His people. Consequently, I didn't know how many more worship songs I could sing without emotion. Inwardly I was crying out for some place to be real, and, finally, sitting in a squad car in the projects of New York, I admitted to myself that the magazine assignments were just an excuse. I had embarked on some sort of spiritual quest to regain my soul and rediscover the heart of Jesus—and that is what had led me to the streets of New York.

Alone and convicted, I felt as naked before God as the man we had just helped down the stairs. Yet somehow I sensed there were even tougher lessons ahead. Lessons that would reshape my faith and change the course of my life—that is, if I could survive the rest of the night.

ChaPter tWo

The Caravan

BMW's, Mercedes and family sedans—some outfitted with car seats—slowly circled the New York City block like hungry vultures looking for road kill at midnight. I pulled away from the caravan and parked our rental car in front of an abandoned warehouse. I could hear music blaring from passing cars and see the length of the street.

On the sidewalk, women of every size, shape, age and ethnicity flaunted their scantily clad bodies, tossed their hair and yelled nasty remarks at the drivers. In turn, the drivers laid their smoldering eyes on each woman until they found one they thought would satisfy their lustful yearnings.

A driver in a late model Oldsmobile pulled up alongside our car, as if to double-park. The man rolled down his window and two young Asian women quickly descended on his vehicle. I noticed he had a gold band on his left ring finger and appeared to be pushing 50.

"Want a date?" one of the women asked.

He pointed at the younger of the two and told her in graphic detail what he had in mind.

"Whatever you want—as long as you pay," said the older woman.

The man flashed a wad of cash and the younger woman jumped into his car.

"Some of these girls can't be more than 18 or 19 years old," I said angrily. "They're selling themselves. And for what—a few bucks?"

I had brought my friend, Steve, along with me to New York for several reasons: He was a good listener, he offered protection, and, most importantly, he acted as an accountability partner. It wasn't that I didn't trust myself or doubted my commitment to my wife. But having a friend with me in each city was the right thing to do.

"It makes you sick, doesn't it?" Steve said as I eased our car back into the caravan.

I felt ill as I watched woman after woman hawk her body to lewd, jeering men. I pulled over to the curb when I saw a lone blonde-haired woman standing below a flickering street lamp, her purse swinging from her shoulder. The woman promptly approached our car as if she were a waitress at a 1970s fast food joint. She couldn't have been more than 19, yet her hollow eyes told a story of abuse and neglect.

"You boys want a date?" she asked in a voice that must have once been laced with fear and hope but now had turned to greed.

I looked into her eyes, unable to respond. Unlike many streetwalkers, she didn't have the mannerisms or markings of a drug addict. It was as if someone had recently pulled her from her home in the suburbs and dropped her on the streets.

Her eyes were like empty wells, but at the same time they

seemed to be begging for more than this life could offer. Instantly, I found myself longing to rescue her, to be the one who rang the doorbell at her parents' home so they could throw their arms around their prodigal and give her all the love she longed for.

As I studied her eyes I couldn't help but think of my young daughters. How devastating it would be to see them working the streets. Desperately I wanted to know who had hurt her and set her on this path to ruin.

At the moment, though, it didn't really matter if her fate had been sealed by her own decisions or if someone else had exploited her. The only thing that mattered was she needed help.

"What's your name?" I asked.

"Cynthia," she replied.

"How old?"

"It doesn't matter."

"How old?" I pressed.

"Old enough," she snapped. "Why, you a [expletive] cop or somethin'?"

"Me a cop? No way," I answered.

I debated if we should take her to a diner, get her something to eat and tell her about Christ's love. Not knowing what would be appropriate, I searched for words to keep the conversation rolling. But before I could speak a man in a red minivan pulled up behind us and began honking—

lust knew no patience. Cynthia glanced at me one last time and read my indecision; then she retreated into the darkness.

I pulled ahead, ashamed I didn't have a plan or the nerve to save her. How could a believer like me help a woman like her? I wondered.

"What can we do for her?" I asked Steve.

"It's a tough one," he said. "Not sure."

Determined, I parked the car and headed back to the corner where Cynthia stood. But after taking a few steps I saw her climb into the minivan and watched as the shadow of the man's arm fell over her shoulder.

"God, help her," I prayed out loud. "Send someone who knows how to help her."

I crawled back in the car and drove toward Times Square. Neither Steve nor I spoke. I seemed to have all the answers for Sunday churchgoers, but I was uncomfortable telling someone like Cynthia about Jesus. At that moment Cynthia didn't need a well-rehearsed sermon. She needed the simple truth of Christ's love, and sadly I found it difficult to find the words she needed to hear. *Jesus spoke to prostitutes; why couldn't I?* I asked.

Though I wanted to excuse myself for not knowing what to say to a streetwalker, my mind's eye could not let loose of her hollow eyes. Cynthia was the first prostitute I had ever encountered and I couldn't understand why, after spending years in church, I was so unprepared and afraid to tell her the truth about Jesus.

Had my pursuit of holiness and fear of sinners kept me

isolated from the likes of Cynthia? I asked myself.

I felt a stabbing pain in my stomach as I realized the answer to my question was yes. I had taken separation from the world to an extreme, mistaking isolation for holiness. In my determination to shield my eyes from the world's wickedness I had neglected those who needed to hear about Jesus. I had run from evil and retreated from unbelievers at the same time. Jesus, on the other hand, was a friend to sinners. He was more concerned with His mission than He was His image.

Condemnation stung me as I reflected on the hundreds of faces I had seen the last two nights in the streets of New York. I could almost smell the blood of spiritually lost people on my hands. There was no denying it: I had elected to be ignorant of the depraved culture because I thought it would excuse me from doing anything to change it. *It was easier,* I thought, *to simply look the other way and pretend millions weren't passing into eternity each year without Jesus.*

The concrete rumbled beneath our car like urban indigestion. The city was teeming with yellow taxicabs and pedestrians as we came upon magnificent Times Square. It was like encountering the Land of Oz—the most recognizable square block in America and the home of Broadway, television networks, and electronic billboards the size of baseball diamonds. To the world it symbolized the coming together of entertainment and capitalism—the basket of dreams America carried on her shoulders. But in the shadows of the gorgeous architecture and neon lights, only blocks away, was another reality. On the backside of all the glitz

and glamour were porn shops and strip clubs—a place where
vagrants, alcoholics, transvestites, hookers and runaways
mingled together in an eclectic mix of hopelessness. Every
temptation known to humankind lurked just yards from
every symbol that gave Americans, and much of the world,
hope.

No longer content to observe the city from the safety of
our car, Steve and I took to the streets. Though we were only
planning to be in New York a short time, I knew God had
more to show me.

Stepping onto the sidewalk my eyes were drawn to a cigar-
toting man in an expensive suit who was emerging from a
sleazy strip joint. Our eyes met immediately. As smoke rose
between the gaps in his teeth, he shoved a flier into my hand
and summoned me into his club for a free drink.

I crumpled the flier, tossed it to the ground, and kept
walking.

"Loosen up, pal!" the man yelled at my back. "Everything
you [expletive] want is inside."

Instantly Cynthia's face flashed in my mind. I spun around
and glared at him. He stopped talking and held my gaze.
I wanted to grab him by his lapels and explain how the
"good times" he was promoting were ruining lives. My fists
clenched and I wanted to deck the man on behalf of fathers
everywhere. But, fortunately, before I could do anything, he
drifted down the street, shoving fliers into every open hand
he could find.

I flipped up the collar of my jacket to stave off the chilly
air. We walked for several blocks and the fury inside me

began to subside. Every few yards steam from manholes and gutters enveloped us and, for an instant, all the surrounding depravity disappeared from sight.

Behind one of the evaporating walls of mist, I spotted what looked like a discarded bolt of fabric. But, as I crossed the street to get a closer look, it became obvious that someone was bundled up inside a thin wool blanket. The man must have heard my footsteps because he peeked out at me then quickly unwrapped as if preparing to defend himself.

His face was framed by wrinkles. His hair was long and matted, his cardboard-brown beard sprinkled with gray. His front teeth were noticeably decayed, his fingernails an inch long. He wore layers of tattered clothing and shoes long dead.

"How you doin'?" I asked, not sure if my intrusion was welcomed.

With bloodshot eyes, he stared back at me but did not say a word.

"You okay?" I continued as if I were a doctor exercising bedside etiquette.

"Yeah," he said, "do I gotta move or somethin'?"

"No, but what's your name?" I asked.

"Barry," he said in a raspy voice. "And that's my buddy Phil."

Introducing me to Phil was Barry's way of telling me he

was not alone. A few yards away, a younger version of Barry rolled out of his blanket and sat up.

"How long the two of you been on the streets?"

Barry looked at Phil as if referring the question to his friend. Neither seemed afraid, but both were curious why two clean-shaven men were asking questions of them.

"We in trouble?" Phil asked

"Nah," I said. "We just want to talk with you. I'm Hal. This is Steve."

"We've been out here a long time," Barry said with a suspicious look. He coughed a few times then wiped his mouth. "Five, six years maybe."

Pulling a candy bar from my pocket I crouched and handed it to Barry. "It's not much, but you guys can share it."

Like a kid on Christmas morning, Barry tore into the wrapper, broke the bar in half, tossed a chunk to Phil and stuffed the rest in his mouth. Though hardened by street life, they still had needs, wants, emotions, feelings and most importantly a soul, I told myself.

My throat constricted with guilt. How many times had I avoided people like Barry and Phil because they made me feel uncomfortable?

"You guys want a slice of pizza?" I asked.

"Yeah," Barry answered. "Pizza and a Coke—"

Steve and I promptly backtracked to a kiosk that sold pizza

by the slice.

Ten minutes later Barry, Phil, Steve and I sat crossed-legged on the sidewalk devouring a late-night snack.

"I've lived all over the place," Barry said, suddenly my best friend. "Welfare hotels, abandoned buildings. I used to stay in New Jersey at one hotel, and it wasn't bad, but it got so [expletive] crazy. People were violent—you didn't know if they'd kill you, even if they had no reason. I had the place stocked with Salvation Army stuff: clothes, a small television set, lamps, tables—and things I got out of dumpsters."

"Why would you leave that for this?" I asked naively.

"They made it [expletive] hard to stay," Barry said regretfully. "That was the end of the road for me—I had no where else to go."

"Do you have family?"

"I don't speak to my family," he said flatly. "I really don't speak with no one I grew up with."

"They probably miss you."

"Not a bit as far as I know," he said, not looking for sympathy. "I ran away from home as a kid. If you'd lived in my home, you'd run away too."

Phil's story was similar and just as tragic. He had hurt his leg, but had no insurance or family to rescue him.

"Look at this [expletive] thing," Phil said, tapping his deformed leg. "I'm a wino now. I drink cheap wine and live out here. It's my claim to fame."

The conversation ebbed as we finished off the pizza and sodas. Suddenly it didn't matter how much money Steve and I made or how little of it Barry and Phil had. And it didn't matter where we lived or the labels society had pinned on us, because for a few moments we were just four men sitting on a sidewalk in New York enjoying one another's company.

"Do you guys have hope for a better future?" I asked.

"Hope!" Phil repeated—insulted. "Don't you?"

"Sure," I replied.

"What a stupid [expletive] question. Yeah, we're bums, but, [expletive], we're still men. If I didn't have hope I'd be in the Hudson River with a brick around my ankle."

"What would it take to get you guys off the streets?" I asked.

"A job maybe, but when you're living in the streets it's hard to keep a job—because you can't stay clean," Barry said. "You can't get any baths."

Without thinking, I handed Barry $40: "Go get a room for the night on us."

Barry stared at the two $20 bills without a word. I couldn't tell if he was grateful or offended.

"You should go to the Teen Challenge center," Steve said. "They're awesome people—they'll help you."

An uncomfortable silence fell on us.

What was my responsibility to these men? I asked silently.

If God had put them in my path, should I take them to the center myself or book them a hotel? Should I pick them up in the morning and take them to a local church? I wasn't sure what to do. So, finally, I settled on leaving them alone and forgetting their names. A hasty departure, I decided, was the only safe course of action.

"One last question," I said awkwardly. "What about God? Have you ever been part of a church or have any Christians ever helped you out?"

Barry weighed his answer before responding. "There may be a God, but I think He gave up on me a long time ago. And, as far as I can tell, churches gave up on me too."

I didn't attempt to refute his statement. Instead I launched into a simple prayer, asking God to watch over them and to meet their needs. Then I extended my hand to say good-bye. Barry's eyes widened, as if years had passed since he had touched a soft, bleached hand. Barry held my hand in his rugged palm until it became uncomfortable. He didn't want me to leave. I wanted to believe it was God speaking to his heart, but that thought vanished when he stammered, "Can we get some more pizza?"

Rain began to rinse the sidewalks shortly after we returned to the car. Pedestrians without umbrellas ran for cover. We wondered if Barry and Phil had escaped the downpour, so we drove back to their patch of cement. But by the time we arrived, they had already retreated to an alley or squat or maybe even a liquor store. I wanted to believe they had taken Steve's advice and headed to Teen Challenge, but I knew the chances of that were slim. Most likely, they were lying somewhere in the cold, shivering, because we had abandoned them.

At that moment I felt guilt's dagger. I had prayed for God to meet their needs when He had already given me the means to help them.

Was I more comfortable with people like Barry and Cynthia roaming the sidewalks like nomads than having them fill empty pews? I asked myself. Was I more comfortable with a sinner going to hell than having one walk into church reeking with alcohol and tobacco?

As the night wore on, an avalanche of accusations aimed at affluent suburban Christians filled my mind. I wanted to indict the entire Church and fault every Christian who had failed to do anything to remedy the plagues of the inner city. It was easier to pin the blame for Barry and Cynthia's demise on haughty believers and snobby churches. But my ranting ended abruptly as I realized how self-righteous I was sounding. I was responsible for my own selfishness and isolation, which had contributed to a religious climate that deemed it acceptable for believers to ignore the likes of Barry and Cynthia. I had no business pointing the finger at anyone else. I had my own issues and failures that I was still working through.

My thoughts retreated to images of a homeless man whom, months earlier, I had passed every day on my way to work. He slept on a bus bench. Even though I recognized the need to offer him assistance, day after day I didn't stop. And one morning he disappeared. I never saw the man again. That experience should have told me something—I wasn't the model Christian I thought I was. But not until I had spent some time in New York did I confront a harsh reality: I had more in common with the Pharisees of the Bible—who evaded the poor—than I did Jesus. They were prideful men who loved their religious traditions more than people. They refused to associate with those who were poor and suffering. Jesus, in turn, condemned their arrogance and priorities. Now I sensed He disapproved of my ways too: I had plenty of pity for the poor, but I wasn't ready to make significant sacrifices or risk my life to offer them hope. As far as I was concerned, that job belonged to believers more qualified and experienced than I.

ChaPter tHree

Hopes and Tears

Every man and woman in the room had a tragic tale that could have inspired a Broadway play and put their name in lights just a few blocks away. The church-run coffeehouse was filled with persons who had suffered neglect, misfortune and failure, which had ushered them down an aisle of despair into the waiting arms of crack and heroin. Their ritual abuse was evidenced by their needle-marred arms and drained eyes. Heartbreak, hurt, insecurity and fear were the burdens that had brought them to their knees and to the edge of death. But something remarkable had resurrected many of them and now they were living in a freedom they'd never known.

Their victory was undeniable and their hope, contagious as they took turns at the microphone. I listened intently as they told their stories—at times feeling like I was watching the ultimate reality television show.

"I thank God for the opportunity to be here and tell my testimony because God is the light in my life," said Marvin, a short black man whose eyes darted back and forth. "God can change anyone and make you a new creation. For four years I was on the streets hooked on crack. Before that I worked at a hospital and thought I had it all."

As Marvin spoke I scanned the room to see if anyone else was as captivated by his story as I was. There were nearly

100 current or former drug addicts who had come for the meeting and free meal. Several sat with arms crossed, dozing. Others stared off into galaxies all their own. But most paid rapt attention, hanging onto Marvin's every word, as if he were revealing a guaranteed formula for making their first million.

"Crack started dragging me down, man," Marvin continued. "I was hopeless. At one point I was living in the Staten Island Ferry terminal, even though I was still working. I was making plenty of money then, but I was so addicted I couldn't even get a hotel room. I'd get back on my feet, go through rehab, but crack always returned."

The men and women seated around me shook their heads as if knowing far too well the addiction Marvin described.

"Every time I'd go back to the street I'd get high," Marvin confessed in a hoarse voice. "I wound up in a halfway house in Brooklyn. It was hell. I'd walk in and hear caps hitting the floor and guys lighting up. The other day I ran into a guy from the house. I told the brother about Jesus and he laughed in my face. Said I had merely gone from one addiction to another and that I was a religious fanatic. I told him I'd rather be a fanatic for Jesus than a fanatic for crack."

Shouting and cheering erupted in the room. Flesh bumps covered my arms as I joined in the applause. It felt good to be in a place where imperfect people were excited about Jesus and telling others about all the great things He had done in their lives. Their message was simple, yet heartfelt and enthusiastic. The meeting wasn't scripted or filled with rituals—just people expressing their gratitude. To them, knowing the love and power of Christ was more important than using the right Christian jargon or debating some deep theological issue.

I couldn't help but admire Marvin. He was not a trained public speaker, but he spoke from the heart about his failures.

"My whole plan was to get cleaned up and back making money at the hospital," he said, ramping up his voice. "I wanted an apartment, a big screen TV and a pimpin' car, but God changed my heart..."

"Amen," someone shouted behind me. "You go, Brother."

"But God said, 'Marvin, you don't need all that. You come work for Me.'" Marvin was almost shouting now. "Brothers and sisters, I don't care about any apartment or TV. I don't even care what's on HBO tonight. All I care about is what's happenin' to you out there on the streets. You don't have to be out there. I'm proof. Open your eyes and look at me. You say, 'I know you—you used to sell me drugs.' You're probably right. But that was then and this is now. I'm here now, thank God. Come in and get your life together. God is able."

Marvin aimed his finger at several people in the audience. "Franklin and Johnny. I see you too, Sue," he said, lowering the volume. "I used to sleep in the trains, in the parks too. Now I sleep in the house of God. I gave my life to Christ and He gives me everything I need. Some of you say, 'I don't have it that bad.' I say, why wait 'til you do? Give your life to Christ now. It never gets better. Do it now."

A man seated near me sniffled and wiped tears from his chin.

Marvin handed the mike over, arms glistening with sweat and eyes ablaze with the fervor of an evangelist. There was something refreshing and penetrating about his words. I felt as if I were hearing the message of redemption and deliverance for the first time.

Another man, inspired by Marvin, grabbed the mike and shared his testimony. He'd been addicted to cocaine, crack, LSD and speed. His family had money, so he'd attended the right college and had the right friends. In the world's eyes he had the perfect life, he said. But pornography and drugs had a stranglehold on his mind until, like Marvin, he found a way out.

"The Lord came down and cleansed me," he said, choking with emotion. "He cleansed my memory of all that pornographic material that was making me sick and insane. He can do it for you too. This is no joke. You need Jesus Christ. Only He can set you free."

He passed the mike to a man laden with tattoos. He resembled a WWE wrestler, his arms and thighs filling out his clothes.

"Praise God for Jesus," he yelled in the mike. "I was on crack. Like a dog with rabies I wandered around not able to find my way home. Life and death didn't matter to me. But I thank God for this place. Many of you know I'm HIV positive. But God is greater than that. He's the God who restores. There's a way out, but you have to trust Him. I'm a living example of it."

Like fans at a wrestling match, the audience cheered.

The leader of the coffeehouse, a Hispanic man with an

intense furrow, took the mike and doled out a tough love speech that I was certain would send everyone running for cover.

"There comes a time when God calls you back," he said, pumping his fist. "When God gives you an open door, come inside. All you've got left is the street or prison. If you close the door on Jesus, you may not get another chance."

Many in the audience shifted uncomfortably, but he had their full attention.

"You guys got to get this straight. You know we're tellin' the truth. But a time is coming for each of you when God will say, 'Enough.' If you like waking up in vomit, go back to the drugs. When you get sick of the muck, the vomit, and the lice in your hair, I'll see you here. Jesus has a lot to offer you. Talk to us before you leave tonight about our Christian discipleship program. Come forward after the meeting so I can pray for you and we'll help you get fed and cleaned up."

He closed his eyes and prayed. When he finished the men and women filed to a window where soup and bread were served. The director set the mike down and stepped toward a group of five men who had come forward to enter the program. By his handshake, I sensed the coffeehouse leader was offering them more than a feeble promise; he was committing himself to their futures. As a group they closed their eyes in prayer and I knew I was witnessing a miracle: the transfer of hope from one human being to another.

I didn't want to admit it, but many months had passed since I had shared my faith in Jesus with anyone. At one time witnessing was a priority in my life. A co-worker once told me he wasn't sure he believed in God or the Bible, but he believed in me. And if I believed in God, he was going to try to serve Him too. That day I led him to Christ. But now stories such as this one were distant memories. I had forgotten the joy of leading people to Christ and seeing their lives transformed. *God isn't giving me many opportunities to share my faith,* I thought, *because He knows I'm not prepared to act on them. Keeping my faith to myself, and not nurturing friendships with unbelievers, has become a way of life for me. Jesus, on the other hand, lived out His message in the marketplace. My faith is being lived out in the company of Christians. I work with Christians, eat with Christians, and do business with them. I'm living in a religious bubble of my own making which makes it nearly impossible to win people to Christ.*

With my elbows propped up on the table, I watched the leader give his five new friends marching orders. *This is where Jesus would be,* I told myself. *He wouldn't run from the HIV-infected, the addicts or the prostitutes. He'd befriend them and say, "Come follow Me."*

A man garbed in an undersized jacket and no shirt underneath slid his tray beside me.

"I'm starvin'," he said, not looking up from his bowl.

"Food looks good," I said.

"You eatin'?" he asked.

"Yeah, later," I replied.

Once the introductions were out of the way, Carlos asked, "If you're not eatin', can you get me another bowl? I haven't had nothin' since yesterday."

"No problem," I said, entering the soup line.

I returned with a brimming bowl and two pieces of bread.

Carlos patted me on the shoulder. "You done good, Boss," he said.

"Last week I came back to God. But I'm still trying to kick the stuff, if you know what I mean."

"God sees where you're at," I said, searching for the right words. "These people are here to help you."

Carlos nodded and shoveled a spoonful into his mouth.

When both bowls were empty, I asked, "Can I pray for you?"

"Yeah, man, I need help."

Embarrassingly, my voice broke and tears gushed down my face as I began to pray: "Lord, Jesus, help Carlos. You know the battles he's facing. But give my friend victory. Help him know he's not alone—that You're with him. Amen."

When I stood from my chair, Carlos rose too. He threw his reeking arms around me as if we were family.

Without lifting his head to look me in the eye, he said, "Thank you, man. I don't remember the last time someone cried for me."

Two hours later, alone in a hotel room, I positioned my head under the shower spigot wishing I could wash away the confusing emotions and haunting faces of the hurting people I'd encountered in New York. Carlos' closing words rang in my ears like a Gregorian chant. I was beginning to understand that our tears matter—that they're a sign to God, and to others, that we care. I sensed God wanted to reintroduce me to the prayer of tears for people who didn't know Jesus. It had been a long time since I had grieved for the millions who are suffering and spiritually lost.

As I lathered in French-milled soap and dried myself with a thick towel, I began to resent the everyday comforts I so easily took for granted—especially when I knew people like Carlos were struggling for their next meal.

It's time that I own up to an ugly reality, I said to myself. *I've been living a pampered life. And because I went without as a welfare child, I think I deserve everything I can get. How much have I spent on things I didn't need just because I could? I've grown so comfortable, I've forgotten what it means to be hungry and thirsty. God has blessed me financially and I've chosen to increase my standard of living rather than step up my level of giving to God's work. Christians like me don't lack the resources to touch the world. We only lack the will and the discipline to tell ourselves no.*

I turned off the lights in my room and crawled into bed. Immediately tears slid down my cheeks onto my pillow. I wasn't sure if I was shedding tears for Carlos, the city, or for the years I had wasted practicing my self-serving brand of religion.

"God, do whatever it takes to transform me," I prayed. "Strip away the pride, fear or prejudice that keeps me from reaching out to people like Barry, Cynthia and Carlos.

Forgive me, Lord. I need Your forgiveness."

Drifting off to sleep an anticipation rose in me for the next leg of my journey—three days in Detroit. But had I known the danger awaiting me in the Motor City, I never would have boarded the plane at LaGuardia in the first place.

"Be strong and courageous.
Do not be terrified; do not be
discouraged, for the Lord
your God will be with you
wherever you go."

—Joshua 5:9

ChaPter fOur

Hookers' Hotel

It was a drizzly evening in Detroit—moonless and foreboding. My friends Eddie and Ken rode with me into a part of the city where prostitutes mingled with drug dealers and gang bangers like housewives do with their neighbors in suburban communities.

The wipers swept the water off the windshield of our rental car as we neared a tiny, rundown hotel. A neon sign directed customers into the front door, and a number of scantily clad girls paraded in and out with their dates. Eddie, Ken and I walked into the hotel's lobby hoping to land an interview.

Flickering fluorescent lights hung above the cramped lobby. They gave everything a bluish hue, including the gaunt-faced man with dark stubble who manned the counter. A cigarette dangled from the corner of his mouth and he reeked with body odor. Before him were stacks of rumpled papers and a large ashtray brimming with cigarette butts.

Like an overeager salesman I told him I wanted to interview some of his girls. The man scowled as if I carried a disease.

"You fuzz?" he grumbled.

"No," I said. "Just gathering some stories."

"For what? You with the newspaper?"

"No."

"Then what the [expletive] are you doin' here?"

"I'm writing some stories for a magazine—but we're not going to use any names."

"Not interested," he said, scanning the pile of papers.

"We're working on a story about Detroit."

"Either you want a room or you don't—I ain't got time for this [expletive]."

He coughed again.

"I'll take a room—one hour."

Ken shot me a nervous glance as I pulled out my wallet.

"How many girls work here?" I asked.

His shoulders slumped as if exhausted by me. "You're either a cop or a priest, aren't you?"

I shook my head.

"Girls rent rooms here just like anyone else. It's none of my business," he snapped.

"How many?" I persisted.

"Maybe 10 or 12 right now," he said. "But I don't know. Don't ask—don't tell. It's none of my business."

"Do they work for you?" I asked.

"No girls work for me or this place," the man snarled. "They do what they do and I do what I gotta do."

"So, are you sayin' you don't know what they do?" I asked.

"These girls are just lookin' for the cheapest place to do their thing. If someone comes here and wants a room I rent 'em a [expletive] room."

Tossing $20 on the counter, I said, "Keep the rest for yourself." He nodded approvingly at his $2 tip.

With key in hand we made our way up the stairs to the second floor. Room 28 had the stench of smoke. Brass doorknobs were battered and scratched and the carpet, soiled. The bed was covered with a thin orange bedspread that had numerous stains and cigarette burns. In the corner was a broken television and the curtains were tacked to the wall.

I left the door slightly ajar, hoping it would be an invitation to one of the girls.

"What do we do now?" Eddie asked.

"I guess we wait," Ken said.

Ken and I looked at one another as if to ask, What would our wives and friends think if they could see us now?

We weren't there more than five minutes when a woman stepped into our doorway and reluctantly leaned in. Another woman peered over her shoulder.

"You guys aren't cops, are you?" the woman asked, her

mouth nearly toothless.

"No, we're reporters from out of town."

Both women wore extremely short skirts, fishnet stockings and long earrings.

"Which of us do you want?" the lead woman asked. "It just depends on what you're into."

"We just want to talk with you," Eddie said.

The women tilted their heads in disbelief. "Tell me now if you're cops," she said, "because I don't want any of that [expletive]."

All three of us shook our heads from side to side. I could feel my face turning red, wondering what my wife was going to say when I told her about this unexpected turn in my itinerary.

"Seriously," I said, "we're doing a magazine story on the city and we just want to talk with you. We won't use your names if you'll talk with us."

"We can do whatever you want but my time costs you," she said. "If I talk, you pay."

"Fair enough," I said. "How much for 30 minutes of your time?"

"Ten dollars apiece—up front," the lead woman said.

I pulled out a $20 bill. The quieter woman grabbed it from my hand and stuffed it down her skirt.

"What's it like being a prostitute?" I asked, sounding more

like a reporter for a high school newspaper.

"Do it for a month and you'll know," the lead woman said, her voice dripping with bitterness.

"How many customers do you have each day?"

"It depends on the day," she said. "But who counts?"

She handed a cigarette to her comrade. Then offered me one.

"No, thanks," I said.

She held one out to Eddie and Ken and they also passed.

"You guys don't smoke either, huh?" she said. "You really did escape from your Boy Scout troop, didn't you?"

I shrugged and smiled.

They laughed openly.

We talked about a wide range of topics: AIDS, pregnancies and the dangers of hooking up with strangers. Each time I tried to bring God into the conversation their answers became short and agitated.

"Why do you do this? There are better things out there for you than this," I said.

The quiet woman spoke up. "It's not exactly what I planned for my [expletive] life, but that's the way it goes. I'll admit—I can't give up the crack [expletive]."

She took a long drag on her cigarette then stared at the wall as if wishing she were somewhere else. They both looked much older than their professed ages of 22 and 24. Their hair was coarse and their lifeless eyes told the tale of women who had been abused, neglected and forgotten. It seemed impossible to me that at one time they were little girls who played with dolls. Now they were playthings for men they didn't even know.

As I listened to the sordid details of their miserable lives, I felt sorry for them. They were human beings caught in a cycle of abuse and despair. This makeshift brothel wasn't exclusive to Detroit—they were in every city. And in each of them there were countless women who sold and abused their bodies for a drug that got them high then abandoned them.

When the 30-minute session neared its end, the soft-spoken woman slumped against the wall and then left without a farewell. Sensing we weren't going to stop her, the other woman darted for the door as well.

"You guys, let's get out of here," I said, wishing I could punch the wall and put an end to the revolting moans coming from next door. "I hate this place ... I really hate it."

Driving a few miles toward a gay bar—where I hoped to conduct some interviews—I couldn't help but feel a little filthy inside. There was nothing appealing about the hookers or their seedy hotel—it seemed more like a portal to hell than a house of pleasure. I wanted to believe the women who turned tricks there every night would somehow find Christ. But it was obvious that the transforming message of Jesus had not yet reached into the brothel. It was as if Satan himself had built a hedge around the place and was keeping the women in bondage.

Lord, I asked silently, *how do we penetrate these places with the gospel? How do we reach people like these two women?* Most Christians like me think it's our job is to connect our community to the church—but maybe we should be equally concerned with connecting our congregation to the culture and the needs in the community. Women like these aren't even on the radar screen for most of us. They've been forgotten. Unless they wander into a church service on their own or flip on Christian television, they may never be confronted with their need for salvation. How do we take the gospel message to them?

Eddie and Ken must have sensed I was preaching to myself because they were unusually quiet. Perhaps they were lecturing themselves as well.

No conversation.

No tunes on the radio.

Just the loud and convicting echoes of our thoughts and the lingering images of two women on a road to destruction.

ChaPter fIve

Guns and Thieves

The party inside the gay bar was in full swing. The bouncer—dressed like a lumberjack—but with a melodic voice, welcomed Ken and me into the smoke-filled club. Techno music pulsated as gay couples, mostly male, gyrated against each other on the dance floor under flashing colored lights.

Off in the shadows, men made out and shared private conversations over drinks and between smokes. The place smelled of stale beer, tobacco and cheap musk. A few men, appearing intimidated, stood on the edge of the dance floor watching. Others looked utterly depressed as they knocked back shots at the bar.

I didn't know what I was getting into when I entered the club, but within seconds I was overpowered by anxiety and apprehension.

My heart pounding, I made my way to an empty table and grabbed a stool. Ken found his own table so customers wouldn't think we were a couple and I'd have a better chance at landing an interview.

Before I could pull out my notebook and pen, a large, middle-aged waiter approached the table.

"Hey," he said in a husky voice. "What you drinkin'?"

"Coke," I replied awkwardly.

"Been here before?"

"No, first time," I said.

"Let me know if you need anything else. My name's Peter."

A few minutes passed before a stranger plopped down beside me.

"I'm William," he said over the booming music.

He looked around the club with a giant smile, his head bobbing to the beat. His brown hair was perfectly groomed and his clothes, expensive. His fingernails were manicured and the gold loops in his ears were small.

"You come here a lot?" I asked.

"Three or four times a week," he said. "This place is hot. You're new here, aren't you?"

"Yeah, from out of town. What do you do for a living?" I asked.

"Accountant. You?"

"Writer."

"What do you write?"

"Books and magazine articles mostly. In fact, that's why I'm in town—doing a story on the city."

"I haven't met a writer in here before," he said with deep

interest.

Instantly I regretted Ken was at a different table.

William scooted closer. I propped my arms onto the table to negotiate some distance between us.

Without warning he patted my thigh. Terrified, I instinctively jumped off the stool and headed for the door.

"What's up?" he said to my back.

I didn't stop to answer. With Ken right behind me, I jetted out the door into the parking lot—knowing I still had 45 minutes to kill before Eddie would be back with the car.

As soon as I caught my breath, regret seized me. I debated whether to go back inside to offer an explanation and share Jesus with William, but I wasn't sure Jesus wanted me there in the first place. It was no place for believers who were weak-kneed and under-prayed.

Jesus was grieved by some of the things He saw 2,000 years ago, I said to myself, *but He endured so His message could advance in dark places. He didn't need to run from anything or anyone. Why did I?*

Ken wandered down the street to a convenience store to grab us some sodas, leaving me alone to my thoughts in the club's parking lot.

A broad shouldered man wearing a dress and heavy makeup approached. His eyebrows were plucked and arching. He wore dangling earrings, a satin blouse, a black mini-skirt and a blond wig. Though thick, his makeup could not conceal his rugged face.

"Hi, what's your name?" I asked, extending my hand.

"I'm Caroline," he replied, surprised.

"Do you mind if I ask your male name, if you have one?"

"Carl," he replied. "But I feel more like a woman, so I go by Caroline when I'm not at work."

"What do you do?"

"I'm a welder."

"How long you been dressing like this?"

"Since I was 9."

"You married?"

"Divorced," he said in an irritated tone.

"Do people mess with you because of how you look?" I asked.

Offended by my question, he turned hostile. "Are you [expletive] messing with me?"

Before I could answer, he reached into his purse, grabbed a small handgun, and coolly trained it on me.

"No," I stammered. "I'm not messin' with you. Just trying to be friendly. Please put that thing away. There's no trouble here."

He looked deeply into my eyes.

I feared I had gone too far—and it was going to cost me my life. I wished I hadn't run out of the club.

"What are you doing out here? You ask a lot of personal questions."

"I'm just checking things out," I said nervously. "I'm a reporter and I'm writing some articles about life in the inner city."

"You gay?" he asked, slowly slipping his gun back into his purse.

"No—married with kids. I'm a Christian journalist. Believe me, I'm not into hurting people or messin' with them."

In a calmer tone, he said, "Christian?"

"Yeah—you go to church?" I asked.

"No. When I was growing up the people at my church said I was going to hell. I stopped going to church after that and never been back."

"That's too bad," I replied.

"Let me give you some advice," he said sternly. "Don't come back here until you're in the [expletive] game."

"In the game?" I asked.

"Until you're gay," he said, as if calling me stupid.

"Hey, I'm going to go catch my ride," I said hastily. "But know this: Jesus really loves you."

"Whatever," he said, throwing his purse over his shoulder

and walking away annoyed.

On the sidewalk, in front of the club, I met a security guard named Joe. He had the gift of gab, and, I had to admit, his uniform alone made me feel a little safer. I told him what had brought me to Detroit—and what I was doing hanging around the club.

He shook his head, saying, "That's some crazy [expletive], man. You reporters will do anything for a story."

Learning that Joe was a native of Detroit, I asked him how the city had changed over the years. He proved to be a knowledgeable historian, full of stories about the auto industry, race riots, and Motown Records. But, in the middle of a story, he went completely silent.

He pointed across the street.

"See those guys over there?" he said, staring at four youths in front of a small liquor store. "I think they're gonna knock that place off."

He spoke without a shred of fear, as if it were just another night at the office.

Meanwhile my pulse raced with panic.

Joe ducked behind a car and called the police on his cell phone.

"[Expletive], get down," he hissed.

I fell to the ground and peeked around the car. My eyes

were drawn to their weapons that were flashing in the white streetlight.

"What should we do?" I whispered. "Nothin'," he said, "unless you're some kind of undercover supercop. I'm paid to be a security guard for this club—not for the whole [expletive] street."

"I hear ya," I said.

The youths raced from the store just as the squad cars arrived. The officers chased the four perpetrators into the shadows of the night. When they were safely out of sight, Joe emerged from behind the car and stepped into the street.

Just then Eddie and Ken pulled up as if driving the getaway vehicle and I flew into the backseat. I didn't stop to say goodbye to Joe or wait around to learn if they apprehended the thieves. "Let's get out of here," I exclaimed. "Too many guns floatin' around here."

Sounding like a fast-playing Dictaphone, I replayed what had just transpired for Eddie and Ken. This was Eddie's hometown, so he didn't appear unnerved by the gun incidents. In fact, he quickly jumped to another subject.

"There's someone I want you to meet," Eddie said. "He's a friend of mine. His name is Irvin and I'm trying to help him shake his habit for good and stay on the straight and narrow."

We drove a few miles to an innocuous brick building, in a dilapidated part of town. The front door opened to a dimly lit hall. The faded red carpet looked like it hadn't been vacuumed in 30 years. And the stench was almost unbearable. I wasn't sure if the building had been abandoned or if some slumlord was charging residents cheap rent. The rooms were more like glorified cubicles, with no formal kitchens.

I spotted one guy fiddling with his crack pipe. And a thin haze of smoke, from something stronger than tobacco, filled the hallway. I cleared my throat as Eddie led us to Irvin's room. My face flushed with fear—we looked too much like undercover cops to be storming into a place like this. I kept my eyes to the ground as if minding my own business. *Besides, there's no telling how many residents are packing handguns*, I told myself, *and I've already seen enough weapons for one night.*

Irvin opened the door slowly and was instantly relieved to see Eddie's face.

"Ed," he announced, throwing open the door.

"Man, I want you to meet some cool friends of mine—Hal and Ken," Eddie said.

Irvin greeted us with a smile and a slap of the hand. He looked more like 60 than 45 because of his years of drug abuse.

"Irvin and I have been goin' to church together and he's gettin' closer to God all the time," Eddie said.

"Eddie helped save my life, man," Irvin said. "He gave me the time and showed me God. I'm a new man."

"You doin' okay with food?" Eddie asked.

"Yeah, gettin' by."

Eddie pulled some money from his pocket and slipped it to Irvin. "Take care, my man. I'm here for you. Call me anytime if you need to talk."

Irvin grabbed his Bible next to his bed. "Eddie gave me this—and I'm doin' my best to follow what it says."

Leaving the building, I felt like hoisting Eddie onto our shoulders and declaring him one of the greatest Christians I'd ever met. He was giving himself away, without fear, so Irvin could have a productive life. Eddie was a modern day Good Samaritan. *If he hadn't stopped and taken the time to help Irvin and nurture him back to health,* I said silently, *Irvin would be one more victim of crack heading to an early grave.*

As our automobile pressed toward a police station for a midnight ride-along, I reflected on what I had just witnessed: drugs, poverty, danger and hope. Most Christians like me couldn't muster the courage to enter Irvin's building week after week. Giving in to fear and playing it safe had become a way of life for many believers. As a result, people like Irvin weren't being reached.

"Eddie," I said, "some of those guys in there are scary. Do you ever worry about what could happen to you in a place like that?"

"Not really, but I don't do anything stupid either," he said. "The way I look at it—it's my job to do God's business; it's His job to cover my back."

ChaPter sIx

A Child's Nightmare

Kyle was a 33-year-old police officer with a 1,000-megawatt smile. His partner, Greg, was clean-shaven and had a full head of brown hair. Either of them could have stepped from the pages of a department store catalog. Their squad car's shiny black seats and dashboard—as complex as an airline cockpit—gave the car a tank-like quality. It felt indestructible and was equipped with enough gadgets to make citizens feel safe—or miserable—depending on which side of the law they were on.

Just as I began to settle into my seat the radio crackled to life.

"It's a domestic abuse call," Kyle announced.

He gunned the accelerator. We weaved through traffic at 55 miles per hour, my body sliding around mercilessly in the backseat.

We heard piercing voices as we entered the driveway. A woman was screaming and a man, yelling as he went, seemed to be chasing her around the house. Kyle and Greg placed their hands on the butts of their guns and glided up the steps. I trailed their heels to the porch. As soon as Kyle knocked on the door the man stopped his tirade, but the woman kept screaming, sensing she had finally gained the upper hand.

"Police, open up," Kyle demanded.

Slowly the door swung open. There, holding the handle was a small girl with a stuffed bunny hanging off one arm.

The girl's mother peeked around the corner, hoping the officers would confirm the coast was clear. The girl's father, dressed in a white tank top and jeans, stepped into view, heaving and sweating, his arms flexed, eyes crazed.

"Daddy tried to kill Mommy," the little girl said.

"Shut up," the man barked.

His eyes flared, then smoldered. Kyle strode into the living room, still poised to draw his gun.

"What's going on here?" he asked the man.

"Nothin'," he replied. "Who called you?"

"I called them," his wife snapped.

The man wheeled toward his wife.

"You [expletive]!" he yelled, before unleashing a flurry of curses.

"You were going to kill me," she screamed back.

"Quiet! Quiet!" Kyle ordered. "You, sir, sit down on the couch—now."

Her hair strung around her face, the woman trembled. Her cheeks were bruised, eyes terrified, and neck bloodied with scratches.

Kyle immediately held his radio to his mouth: "Send backup for transport."

"You're not taking me in," the man said defiantly. "I didn't do nothin'. She's a liar."

"He has a gun," the woman announced.

"A gun—where?" Greg demanded.

"He hit me with it."

"Where's the gun?" Kyle asked.

The woman pointed to the bedroom.

"No, I want him to tell me where the gun is," Kyle said.

The man paused. "It's in there, but I didn't use it."

Greg disappeared then returned holding the gun between his index and middle fingers. Before Kyle handcuffed him and read him his rights, he instructed me to hustle the child onto the porch.

"What's your name, honey?" I asked the small girl.

"Maggie."

"That's a nice name," I said.

"My daddy hit Mommy."

"It's all going to be okay," I said. "How old are you?"

The girl held up four fingers.

"Oh, that's good," I said.

Maggie began to whimper as her dad was led out of the house and wrestled into the rear of a police car. Her mother screamed parting shots.

"I want my daddy," the child cried.

I drew her to my chest and shielded her eyes from her father. In the backseat of the squad car his contorted face was red with anger. Strings of saliva sailed from his mouth as he continued to pitch a fit.

"Maggie," I said, patting her back, "I have a girl at home just about your age. She'd love to play with you. You're such a sweet girl."

She continued to cry.

I looked her in the eye and said, "Honey, I want you to know something. Do you promise you'll remember what I'm going to tell you?"

She shook her head.

"There's a big God up in the sky, in a place called heaven. And He's going to watch out for you your whole life. He's looking at you right now."

"Where is He? I can't see Him."

"I know—but He's there. And all you have to do is talk to Him and He'll help you. Will you remember that?"

She shook her head up and down. "Will He bring my daddy back?" she asked.

Before I could respond her mother yelled, "Maggie, get

your little butt in here."

Maggie nearly collided with Greg as she ran back inside.

"It never makes sense," Greg said under his breath. "Here this guy has a wife and daughter who love him, but he flushes it all down the toilet because he's out of control."

"It doesn't make sense," I replied.

"I hate to say it, but out here it's usually the innocent ones that do most of the crying."

As we drove away, I couldn't help but wonder what Maggie's future held for her. How different her life would be if she were raised in a Christian home, or if some neighbors took her under their wings and gave her a ride to church on Sundays.

My shirt was still damp from the little girl's tears. And, in a strange way, it reminded me that it had been a long time since I had shown any concern for the safety and well-being of kids who weren't my own.

Kyle, Greg and I rode through the streets in silence for several minutes before Kyle said, "I feel for that little girl. What chance does she have?"

"Do you get a lot of calls like this?" I asked.

"Too many to count. And they can turn real crazy in a hurry," he said.

"Have you had any go bad?"

"One almost cost me my life," he said.

"Most people don't know how often you guys put your lives on the line, do they?"

They didn't respond. Not even a nod.

The squad car rolled up to a corner where eight men in their late teens and early 20s were sprawled out on the front steps of an apartment building. All of them were drinking beer, wearing gang colors, and sporting shaved heads, goatees and tattoos.

Kyle and I emerged from the car. Greg stayed behind to work on his report from our last call.

"What's up?" Kyle asked.

None of them answered.

"This guy wants to ask you a few questions," Kyle said, nodding in my direction.

"Nah—we're busy," one replied, lifting a beer bottle in a brown bag to his lips.

"You guys part of the same gang?" I asked.

Again no one answered.

One youth grabbed his beer and shot inside. Another tried to follow, but Kyle stopped him dead in his tracks.

"Where do you think you're going?" Kyle asked.

"I live here, man," the youth said defiantly before disappearing into the apartment.

"What you guys got goin' tonight?" I asked.

"Just hangin' out—no trouble," one of them said with a smirk.

"Yo, hombre," a gang member with a bullet tattoo said to me, "you a cop in trainin' or some [expletive] like that?"

"He's a friend of the department," Kyle said. "That's all you need to know."

"How old are you guys? How long you been hangin' together?" I asked.

Silence. It was obvious the interview wasn't going anywhere.

Kyle broke the stalemate. "You know anything about the shooting that happened down the street last night?"

They shook their heads...disinterested.

After more empty conversation, a perturbed Kyle called it quits. "Later," he announced to the gang members.

Returning to the squad car, he whispered to me, "Either they have something cookin' or they're just not in the mood to talk. But I'd bet they're up to something, and that's not good."

Hours later, sitting on the edge of my bed in a hotel room, memories of Maggie tore at my emotions. I talked frankly to God—in a way I hadn't since my father was killed by a drunken driver. For years I had harbored resentment for losing my father and for having to hear my mother cry herself to sleep night after night, worrying about how she was going to pay the bills. Though my dad's life ended abruptly, he had put his stamp of love and kindness on my life. I had a lot to be grateful for, because my memories of him were good ones. Maggie's father, on the other hand, was leaving a mark of violence and self-indulgence on his precious daughter. Tears soaked my hands as I contemplated Maggie's innocence and her potential fate. It all seemed so unjust for a child to be victimized by her father.

"Protect that child," I prayed with urgency in my voice. "God, give her a loving home where she can be safe or do something to change the hearts of her parents. But please do something; don't let any harm come to her."

As I prayed, I had no way of knowing that in a few days, in Seattle, I would come face to face with more kids who didn't know what it was like to hear a parent say, "I love you."

"At one time we too were foolish, disobedient, deceived and enslaved by all kinds of passions and pleasures…But when the kindness and love of God our Savior appeared, he saved us."

—Titus 3:3,4

ChaPter SeveN

Cobain 'Lives'

Seattle is like a priceless jewel perched on a satin pillow. The rugged, yet verdant Cascade Mountains and the waters of Puget Sound surround the city. In the docks closer to shore, thousands of small sailboats bob gently in the sea-green water, their masts jousting in the wind.

In Seattle, staid and steady adults exist uneasily alongside young people who refuse to conform to anything their parents hold sacred, including religion, status and money. Known as slackers or children of the grunge culture, their religion is whatever whim they choose and their sanctuary is the street.

With fall had come a streak of warm days. Patrons converged on downtown cafes. Seattle's aristocrats frequented boutiques. Middle-class families cheered from the bleachers of Little League games. And troubled young people sat like huddled urchins on the sidewalk.

Steve and I ventured into an area known as Capital Hill where disaffected youth merged seamlessly with the homeless. The kids of Capital Hill had given up on their parents' ideals and lifestyles to roam the streets searching for some kind of satisfying experience.

Steve and I agreed to meet up later in the night. People

were less likely to talk openly if they thought we were undercover cops working in tandem.

Along a wall outside a pub I came upon some teens perched like birds on a wire.

"Have you got any spare change, Mister?" one of the girls called. Her face was smooth and white, but her hair resembled a clump of grass. Half of it was streaked orange and blond, the other half, shaved to a quarter of an inch. Silver hoops pierced her left nostril and eyebrows. Below her eye she sported a tattooed tear.

"What do you need the change for?" I replied innocently.

"To get somethin' to eat."

"Do you live out here?" I asked, rifling my hands into my pockets but coming up empty.

"No, but I spend about 18 hours a day out here."

"All I have are $20s—sorry," I said.

She shifted her attention to other pedestrians. "You have any spare change?" she repeated like a mantra in the wind.

A middle-aged couple simply ignored her.

"Can I please have some money?" she yelled sarcastically. "Doesn't anyone have any [expletive] change in this town?"

A guy with a tattooed barbed wire choker around his neck approached me. "What's up?" he said strangely friendly.

"Nothin' really," I said.

"Just hangin' out on our wall, huh?"

"Yeah," I said, "you from around here?"

"I've been moving around for a while."

"You live out here?"

He nodded and absentmindedly scratched his right forearm. I wondered if he was an addict trying to break his addiction.

"How old are you?"

"Almost 20."

"So why Seattle?"

"There aren't a lot of [expletive] cardboard people here, I guess."

He slumped against the wall and rode it to the sidewalk. He motioned for me to follow his lead, so I did. He pulled a pack of clove cigarettes and offered me one.

"No thanks. Tell me about your family."

"Nothin' to [expletive] tell," he said, taking a long drag on his cigarette. "My parents had a falling out a few years back. They're not together."

He exhaled, sending a thin stream of smoke into the air.

"Divorced?"

The kid laughed out loud. "Yeah, you could call it that. It's a long story. If you have a few days I'll tell you but ..."

"I've got time."

"My mom's a psycho," he said lowering his voice. "But she's not in an institution. You know, she's in all the self-help stuff: books, tapes, 12-step programs, counselors and [expletive]."

The kid sounded hopeless yet optimistic that he'd never make the same mistakes he'd watched his parents make. The way he'd do that, he said, was by making sure he never cared too much about anything.

A girl in her late teens joined us. She sat against the wall with her arms crossed over her knees. She had a Mohawk that was dyed a rainbow of colors. Her voice was so light it might have floated away if the breeze had been stronger.

She and the kid shared the clove.

He swung his arm over her shoulder, pulled her close then kissed her on the cheek.

"Do you two have jobs?" I asked.

They both laughed.

"No way," the girl responded. "What's the use of slavin' for some [expletive] corporation?"

"You do drugs?" I asked.

"We burn," she said, "but avoid the hard stuff."

"Do your parents know where you are?"

"I don't give a [expletive] about my parents. And they don't give a [expletive] about me. I don't think anyone cares about anybody."

"Well, I care," I said awkwardly.

"Who the [expletive] are you? You don't know me. Get the [expletive] out of my face."

Her boyfriend started laughing as they jumped up and left me sitting alone against the wall, feeling like a fool.

With no apparent destination, I wandered down the boulevard. Posters for concerts and movies were plastered everywhere.

Seated at a small table outside a café, I met an 18-year-old who called himself Sims. It took me a while but I finally convinced him I wasn't an undercover cop.

"What about the grunge scene?" I asked.

"The grunge scene is some MTV thing," he said. "If anything, I guess there are kids who are slackers and those who aren't."

"Slackers?"

"Yeah—bedhead, baggy jeans, no job or worries—someone who'd burn with you."

"You a slacker?" I asked.

"Me? No," he said. "I'm all business."

For reasons I hadn't pegged there was something about Sims that gave him an air of sophistication unlike the other kids I'd met. "You seem to be on top of things," I said. "How do you make your money?"

He smiled. "You lookin' to score?"

"Drugs?"

"Yeah—do I look like a [expletive] pimp?" he said with an avenue-wide grin.

"No, I'm not into it," I said.

"Dude, I've got some real sweet stuff here," he said, trying to tempt me.

"So, you're a dealer ..."

"A distributor—it's the occupation for guys like me here in the Northwest. Got to have scratch."

Perhaps unfairly I'd assumed every kid on the street was mindless and in some state of rebellion. But Sims seemed to have chosen a career path—albeit a risky one.

A girl I assumed was Sims' girlfriend stood nearby picking at flowers in one of the café's planters.

"What's your name?" I asked.

"Callie," she said not looking up from the stems in her hand.

"Do either of you go to college or high school?"

"I enroll, drop out, enroll again," Sims said. "Callie here, she's the brains."

Callie shrugged her shoulders. "Right," she said.

"Do you live at home?" I asked.

"Me and my parents aren't close right now, maybe never," she said. "They're way out there."

"Yeah, poor Callie," Sims said sarcastically. "Her parents could own half the [expletive] city with all their money."

"Whatever," Callie sighed.

"Later," Sims said without warning.

"Where's he going?"

"Who cares?" said Callie. "Probably to a party—or to do a deal."

"How long you two been together?"

She bristled, "Me and Sims?" she asked. "No. He's just a guy."

"Are your parents rich?"

"I guess," she said.

An All-American looking kid with a hint of acne and a chip on his shoulder strode up behind Callie and pushed his hands under her shirt.

She threw his hands off her back and cursed at him.

He laughed as he carried on his way.

"Do you know where there's a rave I could check out?" I asked.

"Raves are so over," Callie said, rolling her eyes.

"Are there any parties around here?"

"There's a small one down there," she said pointing. "I used to be into them, but my boyfriend was coming out of one and some guy who was high on speed shot him."

"He died?"

"Yeah, he's gone," she said with a blank stare. "I don't know why it had to happen but it did."

"What happened to the guy who shot him?"

"I don't know," she said. "It wasn't like it was on purpose. He was just out of it."

A grimace briefly stole her face. I sensed she was denying that anything mattered in order to cope with her pain.

"Do you believe in heaven and life after death?" I asked.

She paused. "Yeah, there's something out there. It's probably like having an out-of-body experience—only permanently."

We sat comfortably, letting the unusually warm air circulate around us. We discussed Kurt Cobain, the lead singer of the Seattle-based band Nirvana. Cobain had killed himself at the height of his career. In his death he had become the unofficial spokesman for countless youth.

"Are kids still into him up here?"

"Some. Were you into Nirvana?" she asked.

"No—not really."

"Did Cobain's suicide cause a lot of kids to think about taking their life?"

"Not just because of Cobain. But I guess it's a good way out for some people. I thought about it after my boyfriend died. I wanted to be with him—even if I didn't know where death would take me. But I don't want to get into all this [expletive]. It's way too heavy."

Nevertheless, for nearly an hour we talked about her future, heaven, Jesus, and the way to salvation. She had never been inside a church because they frightened her, she said. She wasn't into a lot of "rules" and "dead" music. And she didn't own a dress. I assured her she could come to church in jeans and sandals, if she wanted. She didn't have to know the first thing about the Bible to step inside a church. God wanted her to come as she was.

"In fact," I said, "I think you'd get into some of the music."

But she wasn't buying it. "I'm not like the Bible people I've met out here. I don't think I really fit," she said with a nervous chuckle.

"Sure, some Christians are into their religious traditions and want everyone to conform. But Jesus isn't offended by our differences or how people look. He's about love and acceptance."

"I'll check into it sometime," she said dryly.

"Churches aren't places filled with perfect people," I continued. "Jesus wants them filled with forgiven people like you and me. Believe me, He isn't angry with us. He loves us and wants everyone to spend eternity with Him in heaven."

I took a deep breath, giving her a chance to toss me a question.

She tilted her head as if crafting one: "Is my boyfriend in heaven?" she asked.

"I can't answer that. I don't know if he knew Jesus?"

"Well, all I know is that I want to go wherever my boyfriend is," she declared.

"Callie, I really hope your boyfriend is there, but if he's not, I guarantee you—if he could—he'd beg you to accept Jesus so you could live forever in heaven. You can accept Jesus as your Savior right now. You can repeat a prayer after me if you like. Talking to Him is as simple as talking to me."

She paused. "I'll check it out sometime, but I want to do it alone, when I'm ready."

When it was time to leave, I scribbled the name of a church in the area on a piece of paper and handed it to her. Somehow I knew it was only a matter of time before Callie went to a church, so I prayed that God would lead her to one that didn't frown on blue jeans.

I reconnected with Steve and we descended into a basement to observe the party Callie had told me about. The music, dark-lit room and damp walls made me feel like I had entered a dungeon of pleasure—where you checked your inhibitions and identity at the door. Couples, seemingly joined at the necks, could be seen everywhere. Dozens of youths sucked pacifiers and lollypops to prevent them from biting their tongues in their drug-induced daze. Some were slumped against walls, their heads bobbing. Others bounced like witch doctors on the dance floor.

A youth grabbed my arm and yanked me into the gyrating mob. The amplified music ripped through me like electrical current. I shook myself loose and put my fingers to my ears to mute the noise. It was obvious I couldn't hold a conversation above the music or tape any interviews.

"Steve, let's get out of here," I shouted.

He couldn't hear me, so I simply pointed to the door. He nodded that he understood.

We hiked to a square near the water's edge that acted as the center of Seattle's somewhat ambiguous downtown. It spanned only one city block and was full of mature trees with gnarled, above-ground roots.

Walking along the perimeter of the park, I poked my head in a few specialty shops. There, on a corner, I met a young black man handing out gospel literature.

"God bless you," he said time and again. "Read this, you'll be glad you did."

He wore black sweats, purple and white tennis shoes and a green windbreaker. He stood in one place rather than pursuing people with an outstretched arm as many street evangelists do.

He handed me a salvation tract. In turn, I told him I was a Christian. He gathered his literature in one hand and gave me a high-five.

"Good to meet you, Brother," he said. "My name is Wayne."

At one time he was hooked on drugs, he explained, but with God's help he conquered his addictions. Now, he came to the streets most nights so others could have the same peace and freedom he found in Jesus.

A 14-year-old named Brian came from nowhere and invaded our conversation. Though he had a high-pitched voice, he seemed much older and street tough.

"Hey, Brian, where you been?" Wayne asked.

"Man, don't be askin' me that," he said before laughing.

"He's coming off a high," Wayne explained.

"What the [expletive] you talking 'bout 'high'? I'm not high, I'm normal: I'm stoned."

Wayne leaned over and whispered to me that Brian was on his own—his mom and dad were deceased.

"Don't you know—I'm the devil's son?" Brian said as if it were a joke.

"Don't say that, dude," Wayne said.

"'Cause I hustle tricks, even with men, and I do drugs and ...," he mumbled like a drunk, before giggling again.

"Where do you live?" I asked.

"My caseworker is tryin' to get me off the streets, but I haven't seen him in a week so I don't know what the [expletive] is going on."

"So you sleep in an alley or open car somewhere?"

"Whatever ... wherever," he said. "I don't worry about it, 'cause no matter where I am I can take care of myself." Suddenly going sober, he added, "I got this with me."

He retrieved a switchblade from his pocket and popped the six-inch blade.

I knew God was working on my heart, because I was beginning to see Brian as a person with real needs rather than a punk to be avoided. He wore his feelings of betrayal and abandonment on his sleeves. I couldn't imagine living on the streets at his age and selling your body so you could eat. I couldn't imagine the teenager's lonely and desperate nights.

"Brian, listen to me," Wayne said. "You need to get into a program that can get you off the streets. Let us make it happen for you."

Brian dismissed his advice. "I'm okay. Leave me [expletive] alone."

We shook our heads in disappointment and turned to walk away.

"Find me when you're ready," Wayne said.

Brian's tough exterior melted.

"I didn't mean it," he said. "Man, you guys are cool dudes. Let's hang for a while."

I looked at Brian and my heart sank. He needed a father to put his arms around him and tell him he had value. He needed a mother who would pray for him and tell him she loved him.

"I'll tell you what, Brian," Wayne offered. "I'll walk with my friends up the street, then come back and we'll talk some more. They have to meet some cops for a ride-along."

"That's cool," Brian said, though obviously wondering why we were hanging with the police.

"Brian," I added, "take care of yourself and hang close to Wayne. He'll show you what you need to do. For starters, I'd recommend you stash the blade. It's liable to get you hurt."

Like a kid returning stolen milk money, he bit his lip, sighed emphatically and reluctantly handed the knife to Wayne.

I admired Wayne's humility and passion for reaching people for Christ. He wasn't interested in having his face on Christian television, owning a big title in front of his name, or collecting huge offerings from churches. I even sensed his discomfort when I slapped him on the back and praised his ministry. He was simply grateful to God for saving his life, and he wanted to show his appreciation by working for God to reach others. Wayne didn't own a business card or have a brochure or DVD trumpeting his ministry. He said God hadn't called him to establish a ministry-business; He had called him to tell others about the Savior's love. So all he needed was a Bible, some gospel tracts, his testimony and a genuine smile.

I was thankful God had introduced me to Wayne before

I left Seattle. In a few short hours, like an angel delivering a personal message, a total stranger had shown me the difference between a professional Christian and an authentic follower of Christ. Wayne, I decided, didn't need business cards that bore his name and a lofty title after all. He had "Follower of Jesus" written all over his life.

Miam

"The poor are shunned even by their neighbors, but the rich have many friends. He who despises his neighbor sins, but blessed is he who is kind to the needy."

—Proverbs 14:20,21

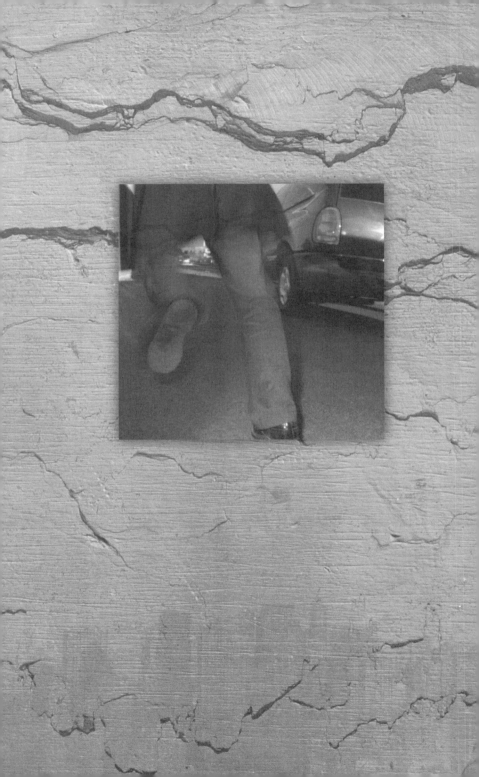

_____

ChaPter EIght

The Chase

The boy flashed a smile as his father handed him a Miami Heat basketball pennant. He admired it for a second then said with a whine, "I want a jersey too. Dad, get it for me—okay?"

"We'll see—maybe after the game," the irritated father replied.

My eyes scanned the massive sports arena. Fans everywhere munched on foot-long frankfurters, tubs of popcorn and trays of chips drenched in melted cheese. Thousands of families and couples had ventured from the suburbs to enjoy a night of NBA action. I had to admit that rubbing shoulders with fellow basketball fans was a much-needed diversion. I needed a break from the pain and poverty of the inner city. The people sitting in my section wore nice clothes and most likely drove expensive cars and lived in upscale communities. I felt right at home with this crowd.

But following the game, riding with the police on the midnight shift, I knew I was going to experience a different side of Miami.

Three hours later, my legs carried me as fast as they could

through the darkness of an empty parking lot. I don't know if it was adrenalin or fear but I was stride for stride with a Miami police officer chasing two men who had crashed a stolen car into a store window in a burglary attempt. The officer, Cortez, called such crimes "smash and grabs."

"Need backup!" he yelled into his shoulder mike. "Suspects on foot; I'm in pursuit."

"Stop! Police!" he yelled into the air. "Stop! Police!"

As we ran I wondered if I had lost my mind. Sure, I was wearing a bulletproof vest, but I also had a wife and children at home. At any moment these thugs could wheel around and start firing at us and there was nowhere to hide.

Cortez showed no signs of slowing so I gasped for air and leaned into the darkness. The rhythmic sound of our rapid footsteps ricocheted off the pavement. I felt like I was starring in an episode of *Cops*.

Suddenly the officer stopped in the shaft of orange light coming from a street lamp.

"[Expletive]," he yelled as he secured his gun, "we lost 'em." A string of curse words flowed from his mouth. Meanwhile I tried to catch my breath. Now that the chase was over, part of me was grateful we hadn't overtaken the culprits. If we had, I'm not sure what I would have done. After all, a lesson in hand-to-hand combat wasn't a prerequisite for my ride-along.

Back in the squad car, Cortez maneuvered through a depressed neighborhood that thousands of people called home. Some were immigrants; others had simply gambled on the American dream and lost. Clotheslines hung with tattered T-shirts and underwear. Broken down cars clogged side streets. And merchants defended their stakes with alarms and iron bars.

He drove to the rear of an abandoned building and we climbed metal stairs to the gravel roof.

"I got a tip that there's a crack house across the street," he said. "We should have a bird's-eye view from up here."

He kept his body low, almost crawling to the ledge. I mimicked his every move.

Poking his head above the rim, he motioned for me to join him. "There it is," Cortez said. "We're going to stake out the place to see what kind of action it gets."

The porch lights revealed two cars parked in the driveway. Predictably, we watched three more cars pull up and make brief stops.

"It's like a drive through," I said. "When will you guys bust it?"

"That's a decision someone else will make. But, believe me, we'll nail these guys."

Cortez was a nervy Caribbean immigrant fulfilling his lifelong dream of being a cop. He had short black hair and a pencil-thin mustache. Though he'd only been on the force for four years, he was no longer enamored with police work: A close buddy had been killed in the line of duty.

From our vantage point on the roof, it appeared that

Miami's youth owned the streets. They loitered in a convenience store parking lot where signs warned them away. In small groups they strutted down the boulevard and huddled around low-riding automobiles.

"Do the kids have respect for the law?" I asked.

"A lot of 'em don't have respect for anything. But many of them are salvageable—though sometimes it takes something tragic to get them on the right road."

"Tragic?"

"Yeah, like the death of a brother or buddy."

"Or jail time?" I asked.

He nodded. "Time to go," he said. "I've seen enough to report to the sergeant."

Later that night, when Cortez spotted a suspicious-looking man, he slammed on the brakes and jumped out of the vehicle.

Spotting the squad car, the man turned and headed in the opposite direction.

"Come back here," the officer hollered like a drill sergeant. "Get back here now."

The man pivoted and began tiptoeing toward us.

"Where you going?" Cortez snapped.

"I don't know," he replied.

His hair was dyed platinum-white and his face was covered with thick powder. His fingernails were long and pink and he had silver hoop earrings in both ears. His voice had a soft, sensual quality.

"What's your name?" Cortez asked.

"Danny—have I done somethin' wrong?"

"Not yet," the officer said. "But the night's young."

Just then a resident ran up to Cortez begging for help. Cortez departed hastily to deal with a disturbance. "Hal, hang here—I'll be back. You stay here too," he called to Danny.

His body shaking, Danny wrapped his arms around himself.

"Are you sick or are you just coming off something?" I asked.

"I'm sick."

"Flu?"

He paused. "No—more serious. I have AIDS."

I was stunned to silence.

"You serious?" I finally asked.

"That's not [expletive] that someone makes up."

"I'm sorry—does your family know?" I asked.

"Mom doesn't. Dad does, but I don't think he was

shocked. He thinks all of us deserve what we get. He kicked me out when he found out I was taking female hormones."

I shielded my disgust and sadness.

Without warning heavy rain began to fall and Danny and everyone else ducked under overhangs. An unknown desperation for Danny and the lost souls of Miami broke inside me like a dike. I drifted to the street corner to be alone. Strangely I raised my hands, tilted my head, and stared straight into the eyes of heaven.

"God, what's happening here? These people are dying. They are lost and going to hell unless we do something."

I paused as if waiting for an answer. The rain continued to drench my clothes and hair, but it didn't matter.

"God, please hear me," I yelled, fighting back the tears. "What do You expect from me? These people are desperate for help. Someone has to help them. What can I do?"

Like a scene from an old black and white movie, I stood on the corner with my arms outstretched. Raindrops continued to fall from the heavens, but no answers fell with them.

chaPter nIne

Killer at 16

David looked and acted the part of a gangbanger. He wore baggy jeans and a white tank top, and had a gold chain dangling on his chest. His neck and arms sported tattoos with hidden meanings, and his hair was gelled to a crisp.

He stood with his shoulders back, his chest out, his spine sentry-straight and his chin raised.

A worker with the juvenile system introduced me to David; then he left us alone at a fast food joint. David had agreed to be interviewed as part of his rehabilitation program.

"Thanks for agreeing to meet with me," I said.

"Let's make it quick," he said, slamming his cell phone shut. "What the [expletive] do I need to be talkin' to you about?"

"I flew here to do a story on someone like you—I'm not using real names—just stories. Can you help me out?"

"Like some magazine sh— or something?"

"Something like that."

His scowl gave way to a slight grin. His well-defined arms relaxed and I breathed easier. "Go for it," he said.

He told me he was 16, though he could have passed for someone 10 years older. Short for his age, he had the face of a scrappy prizefighter.

"What are some of the things you've done for the gang?" I asked.

"Straight up? No names?"

"You have my word—no names."

He paused.

"If you use this [expletive] against me, I'll come after you."

I didn't flinch. "After tonight you'll never see me again—promise."

He weighed his answer.

"I've done drive-bys, robberies, drug runs, been on lookout. But not anymore."

"You kill anyone?"

"When you do a drive-by you don't look back to see if anyone is down. All I'll say is that I fired some shots."

Somehow I knew he was lying. "So are drive-bys your thing?"

He shook his head from side to side as he shoved a handful of fries into his mouth. "I do tattoos for the gang and watch over our girls."

"Girls—you mean hookers?"

"What else?" he asked with a demeaning chuckle.

"And you're 16?"

He cleared his throat—"Yeah."

"How many girls you watchin'?"

"Three of 'em on the street tonight. Hey, I can hook you up."

Ignoring his offer, I asked, "How much do you make in a night?"

"Usually $250 to $300."

Once he grew more secure talking to me, he confided that he'd recently had a "gig" with a rival gang member.

"I was doing a tattoo at the time," he said. "I had no shoes on and I open my door and here is this dude who I pimp-slapped across the mouth earlier in the day. He came back for [expletive] revenge with some of his homies. I slammed the door and made it to my kitchen and grabbed a [expletive] knife. I shoved it at the [expletive]."

David laughed at the memory.

"Dude was scared," he continued. "But said he'd meet up with me later so we could settle it. Guess that's the way it's got to be because I couldn't take on all of them [expletive]."

One more question, I said: "Do you believe in God?"

"My mother is religious," he replied without hesitation. "But I don't think the Dude up there wants anything to do with me except to throw me in jail."

Suddenly a pager on David's belt went off. He eyed the display screen.

"Gotta go, my man," he said. "One of my girls. She may have a freak on her hands. Next time you're in Miami, come by and I'll give you a free tattoo."

It was just past midnight when Steve and I found a park teeming with young people. As we walked through the park we were pummeled with obscenities. On a bench in the heart of the park two girls sat smoking cigarettes. Both were pretty and hid their thin frames under baggy clothing.

They figured we were either there to solicit them or we were cops looking to make a bust.

"We get guys like you rolling down here from the 'burbs lookin' for skanks all the time," said one of the girls. "But we don't go with no one so get the [expletive] away from us."

"That's not our deal," I said. "Actually I'm a reporter doing a magazine story on the city. Do you mind if I ask you some questions?"

They both shrugged.

I pulled out my pen and notebook hoping to convince them that I was the real thing.

Until a week ago they had been living with a friend but had been kicked out by the landlord. Grace was 16 and Tonya was 17. They had both dropped out of school and were raised in broken homes. Now their gang was all the family they had.

"If you're alone and someone jumps you, you know you have a gang to back you up," Grace said. "It's like having insurance—you have someone you can turn to in any [expletive] situation."

"Is the gang more important than your real family?" I asked.

"What's real about my [expletive] family?" Tonya replied.

To get into the gang, they explained, each of them had to be punched by other gang members for 18 seconds. They also had to let one gang member beat them up every day for six days. "They gotta know you can take it," Grace said. "If you can't you're not gonna make it."

Grace left home because her mom died. Tonya ran away because her mom beat her. Both expressed a desire to leave the streets and the gang, but they said the likelihood of that happening anytime soon was doubtful.

Tonya pulled out a new cigarette and lit up. She took a long drag and passed the pack to Grace.

"What do you want to do with your life?" I asked.

"I want to be a clothes designer and a lawyer," Tonya said bluntly.

"How about you, Grace?"

"I wanna ... I don't know what I want to do," she said. "I'm just worried about tonight. After that, I'll think about what I wanna do with the rest of my life."

"What advice would you give girls your age who are thinking of running away?" I asked.

Grace thought hard about her answer. "If they have problems they should try to work them out at home because it's easier to do it there than out here on the streets. People think, 'Oh, I'll go live on the streets and have my freedom,' but that's not the way it works. You go to the streets and you worry 24/7: Where I gonna stay? What am I gonna eat? Are the police gonna look for me? It's totally jacked up."

"What she's sayin' is that life is [expletive]," Tonya said, her voice laced with bitterness.

I wanted to assure them things would get better, but I had serious doubts that they would. These girls were targets. They'd be fortunate to live to see their 21st birthday. Chances were their families had already seen them for the last time. Without a miracle, these girls would be sucked deeper into gang life, used for prostitution, and turned on to drugs.

After interviewing Grace and Tonya, I wanted to withdraw to a hotel room and unload some thoughts on my Powerbook. But I had made arrangements with a social worker to ride along with an organization that rescued wayward kids from the streets.

Anthony, the director, was easygoing and we made quick work of becoming friends. He cautioned that what I was about to see would turn my stomach.

"What do you mean?" I asked.

"I'm takin' you to where we're trying to help some teenage male prostitutes," he said. "We're tryin' to get them off the streets, but the big dogs throw their money at these kids and they can't break away from the lifestyle."

"Big dogs?"

"Yeah—switch hitters if you know what I mean. Boys sell themselves to older men."

When he said that, an image of 14-year-old Brian back in Seattle flashed in my mind.

Anthony eased the van into a dark parking lot on the fringes of a greenbelt. I winced as I watched several boys wave down cars and compete for a trick.

Anthony pointed to a yellow Cadillac that was circling like a hungry shark looking for food. Finally, the car stopped near one boy who was sitting on a bench. Seeing the Cadillac the boy glanced in both directions then made his way to the car and hopped inside.

Anthony and I sat in the darkness watching the travesty unfold.

"What do you do to help them?" I asked.

"We get to know them. Our people get out here before the show is in full swing and we try to talk them into letting us feed them dinner and find them a place to stay. We try to do all we can to give them an alternative to selling themselves."

"What do the police do about this?"

"They set up stings," Anthony said. "They do all they can

to clean it up, but it doesn't take long before the players are back in action. I've worked down here for three years and it still makes me sick."

"Why don't you just go pick them up?" I asked naively.

"You can't force them into the van. You're asking for trouble—because some of these kids are owned by bosses or pimps. They have to come with us on their own. Don't worry, our team will make the rounds again tonight and each of these kids will be given a chance to get out of it."

Anthony turned the ignition to leave. And, just as he predicted, the sight of these lonely kids hawking their bodies turned my stomach.

Suddenly, despite the soothing palm trees, sun-drenched beaches and tantalizing ocean views of South Florida, I couldn't wait to board the plane for Chicago and leave this American tragedy behind.

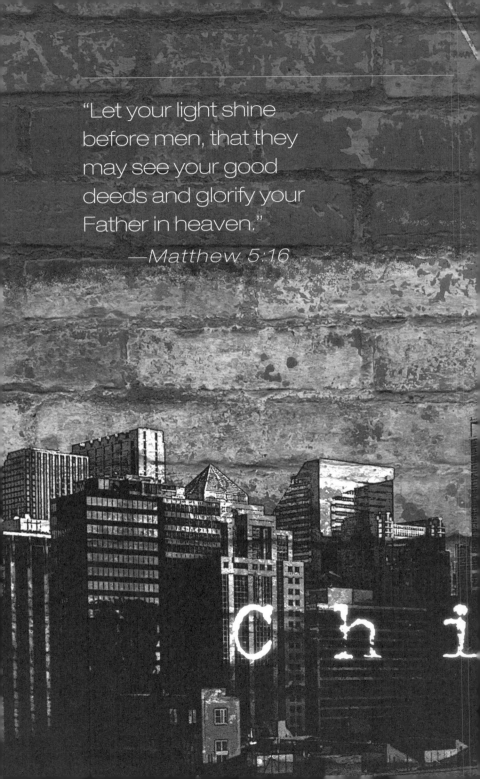

"Let your light shine before men, that they may see your good deeds and glorify your Father in heaven."

—*Matthew 5:16*

ChaPter TEn

Gangland

Chicago bustled with activity as my rental car entered the pristine downtown area. Men and women in business suits herded toward the subway, returning to the suburbs for the night. In-line skaters cut through parks. Students with backpacks at the University of Chicago clogged walkways. And joggers ran in pairs along magnificent Lakeshore Drive, parallel to Lake Michigan.

I ventured onto the Navy Pier, trying to kill some time in the amusement area before my ride-along with the Chicago police later that night. Sitting on a bench and shooing pigeons from my sandwich, I marveled at the tall skyscrapers whose reflections shimmered against the small waves that lapped the city's border. I was awestruck by the vast array of glass and marble edifices—mixed with older buildings of brick, arches and mortar.

The air was filled with the laughter of children taking in amusement rides. Young couples, arm-in-arm, romantically paced the pier. A grandfather-type shared popcorn with a small boy. For a few hours, I didn't want to believe there was an underbelly to beautiful Chicago.

I hopped back in my car and tuned the radio to a 24-hour news station. Immediately the harsh reality of the city hit me when details of a homicide were reported. That story was followed by one about a kid being thrown to his death off the top of a building. For a moment, I debated whether to proceed with the ride-along. *Maybe I should sit this one out,* I said to myself. *Maybe I need to head home altogether.*

But, by 10:30, after circling the block a few times, I parked the car and entered the police station.

Jack, a proud Chicago cop, had an appetite for discipline and justice. His handshake was as fierce as his voice. Like a good soldier Jack walked with a straight back and chest out. His military training had proved invaluable on the streets of Chicago where he had traded gunfire with gangbangers. Recently he'd been forced to shoot a perpetrator, but he refused to talk about it.

"It still gets to me," he said honestly. "I can't grow numb to it. That would be to sacrifice the person I am for the badge, and that's not what this job is about."

As Jack laid down his philosophy on life, Tina, his partner, assumed her position in the squad car.

We crept into the street in our fortified vehicle, edging toward the neighborhoods that made up Jack and Tina's beat. As we left the precinct we passed downtown businesses, then traditional homes with immaculate facades. But beyond that—just minutes away—the projects entered our view. Some of the buildings appeared to be gutted and half-lived-in.

"Are gangs a big problem here?" I asked.

Jack glanced at me to make sure my question was a serious

one. Then he bailed me out by offering valuable information: "Yeah, it's a problem. But one thing we have going for us at night is that gangs like to be seen. So when it's dark a lot of them keep to themselves, sit around in their apartments and get drunk."

"Do you know how many gang members there are in the city?" I asked as we drove toward what Jack called "a dangerous neighborhood."

"I've heard different numbers. Once another partner and I were patrolling a few blocks from here and all of a sudden we heard bam-bam-bam, pow-pow-pow," he said, his voice echoing off the windows and drilling into my ears. "That night the entire street was like a firefight in Vietnam. It was …"

He cut his story short and pointed. "Down this street we have two gangs living in their own little world. When they decide to scrap with one another, the guns come out. The walls around here are pockmarked with bullet holes."

It was difficult to imagine a place where gang members stuffed guns in their pants as nonchalantly as businessmen carried wallets in their pockets.

Jack pointed to an unassuming house with a porch swing and a small lawn. I shook my head in disbelief. It didn't fit my image of a hub of gang activity. Instead it resembled some of the houses in my own neighborhood.

"We have to be very careful when we come in here," he said, lowering his voice to emphasize his point. "We've got several squad cars patrolling these streets tonight. Otherwise it's just bang-bang-bang."

Peering through the windshield, I noticed another squad car lurking in the neighborhood, cruising slowly. The area was well canvassed, Jack said, but no one could really be sure everything was under control. It was like a contested border where the factions went back and forth at one another, claiming and reclaiming territory.

After giving my eyes a chance to wander, Jack said, "One time we responded to a party and told them to break it up. We found two guys with full-blown automatic weapons."

"Any police deaths?" I asked a little too casually.

Jack and Tina were silent for a moment.

"Not recently in our area," Jack said after clearing his throat. "But in another part of the city."

They fell silent again, as if honoring a fallen comrade.

We turned a corner and eventually came face to face with Lake Michigan, a vast body of water more characteristic of an ocean. The lights of small sailboats dotted the water like stars. It was an unforgettable view, just miles away from one of the city's fiercest areas.

Our squad car pulled into an area that was once a high-class neighborhood in the 1920s and '30s, but now it had a reputation for crack dealing. A man cursed at us from a second floor window, his arms flailing so much I feared he would fall out.

"Drugs," Tina proclaimed disgustedly.

I nodded as the man continued to sway.

Tina and Jack dutifully ignored him.

"Gangs are the biggest problem here," Jack said. "The whole gang structure breaks down into geographical areas, then it branches out from there into individual affiliations at the neighborhood level. There's different terminology across the country: 'Sets' in some places—'pits' in others. Each gang has its own personality, just like any other social club. Some recruit members as young as 6 and 7 years old."

"Other gangs are different," Tina interjected. "They try to keep their members limited to 13 or 14 as kind of a prestige thing. They're very big on prestige and honor. It really doesn't surprise us to see hardcore gangbangers before kids turn 13."

We passed a park where stark, leafless trees crowned a small cement monument. Bushes were bare and the grass, wilted. Nature, it seemed, had thrown up her hands and chosen not to fight back.

"Do you hate the gangs?" I asked.

"Actually, no," Jack said. "I hate what they do, but gangs are not just nameless, faceless things. Gangs are people going in the wrong direction. All these kids are redeemable but people like me can only do so much."

"What can we do to curb gang activity besides just busting them, throwing them in jail, and watching them shoot each other?" I asked as we glided to a stoplight.

"Basketball leagues and other city-sponsored programs are doing a pretty good job," Jack said. "I'd much rather have a kid pulling the trigger on a jump shot than pulling the trigger on a handgun. But with all they live with, you can almost understand why they feel they need to be in a gang. There's power, prestige, women, money, respect. Gangs offer everything they want—they just have to pay a higher price for it. And sometimes that price is their lives or prison."

"Is there any part of the city you just won't go into?" I asked.

"No," Tina said firmly.

"We can't give up any turf," Jack said. "We can't relinquish any ground. If we do—we lose."

At daybreak, Jack and Tina dropped me off at the precinct before they made their final rounds. The sun's rays were knifing between skyscrapers and my eyes were fighting to stay open. It had been a long, but enlightening night.

As I drove toward my hotel, I couldn't escape the sad reality that Christians had given up ground to the enemy. *We've been content to watch the demise of our cities from a distance,* I said to myself. *Many of us have viewed them as objects of God's judgment and punishment, and simply thrown up our hands. But God hasn't given up on them. We're the ones who've been unwilling to pay the price to bring light to these dark places. God wants to save these gang members. It's His heart to forgive and restore. None of them are beyond reach. If we give up on them, we're giving up on God.*

I cut my sermon short, realizing I was beginning to sound more like an evangelist than a reporter. But it was obvious

God was restoring my hope for our cities and showing me
they could be reborn if believers like me were willing to be
used by Him to rebuild the lives of desperate people.

ChaPter ELeven

Children of Sorrow

The Sears Tower antennae jutted above a layer of haze
like nuclear missiles poised for a retaliatory strike. I passed
through one neighborhood that, at first, looked like it had
taken a direct hit. But actually the demolition activity was
part of the city's beautification initiative.

On the way to an interview with the pastor of a church on the
south side, I passed white children in colorful school uniforms
playing dodge ball on an asphalt playground. A shoeless old
man in an ankle-length coat stared at them through a tall
fence—but he was quickly chased away by the yard monitor.

Fifteen minutes later I entered the predominately black
neighborhood where the church was located. The residents
had obviously taken pride in caring for their homes and
yards, but it was a far cry from the deep sculpted lawns
and ash-white sidewalks of the rich and famous. There
were no Wal-Marts with wide aisles and soothing music on
the intercom. There were no fancy restaurants or upscale
shopping malls. This was a tight community that had learned
to be content with a simpler life.

I drove slowly to avoid some children in tattered shoes
tossing a football in the street. It struck me that the kids in
this game weren't as fortunate as the ones donning school
uniforms across town. *At this age, they probably don't know*

what the other kids have—large screen TVs, X-Box sets
and community swimming pools, I thought. But, as they get
older, some of them may be lured into selling drugs so they
can taste the fruit of prosperity.

Once an area where kids could be shot by stray bullets or
be recruited by drug pushers, the community had made great
strides since Pastor Jones and his wife, both African-Americans,
had arrived. Now, largely because of their congregation's
influence, the neighborhood was a much safer place.

When I introduced myself to Pastor Jones in his office,
instantly I sensed he was the kind of man who had learned to
accentuate victories and not back down from any challenge.
For him, surrendering turf to the enemy wasn't an option.

"Tell me how God brought you here," I said.

"I was drawn here," he said smiling. "I grew up on a farm
in Missouri. When I visited the city for the first time, I fell in
love with it."

He nurtured the romance summer after summer, making
numerous trips to the city. His parents, meanwhile, expressed
concern because they saw Chicago as a place where "country
folk" went to die violent deaths. But after serving in Vietnam
and graduating from college, he moved to Chicago and
became the pastor of the church, which had since grown to
more than 1,000 members.

"Brother, let's get out of the office for a while," he said.
"The problems aren't in this room and neither are the
solutions. There's a young man I'd like to introduce you to."

He walked briskly down the street, like an athlete in

training. He greeted neighbors with both hands as if he were mayor. It was obvious that, to them, he was more than a politician; he was a spiritual leader and an advocate for anyone who needed help.

A fast-talking woman stepped into our path. In excited and urgent tones, she described a plumbing problem at her house.

"Did you turn off the water?" he asked.

"Yes, Pastor."

"Sister, give me an hour and someone will be there to help you."

"Bless you, Pastor!" she said with a wide grin.

"Do you get a lot of requests for help?" I asked, as we proceeded down the street.

"Yes—that was a single mom," Pastor Jones replied. "We see it as part of our mission here. We believe God wants us to pastor the entire community, to do everything we can to show people that Jesus cares about their needs and so do we."

A few blocks down we arrived at a simple brick house. A young man appeared at the door. "Hi, Pastor," he said, beaming.

"Sean," Pastor Jones said, "I brought someone with me who'd like to hear your story."

Without pausing, Sean broke into his testimony: "I was born not far from here—right down the road. I started getting involved in bad stuff at the age of 6 or 7. I was smoking cigarettes, marijuana, drinking.

"My sister was going out with this guy and I wanted to impress him. He was the one who taught me how to steal. My parents would have parties every weekend at the house and they thought it was funny to see me get drunk. They didn't know it was a preview of my future.

"I got more violent. I was 11 when a friend asked if I wanted to join a gang. My brothers and sisters were already in a gang. When I was 8 years old my father left us. It hurt me real bad, so I grew up wanting to hurt other people.

"I went in as a foot soldier, the lowest level of all. A foot soldier is the ground level, where the young kids start out. You're on the front lines, doing the dirty work: stealing things, running drugs, being a lookout. Once you've been in it long enough and proven yourself, the first advancement you make is to spokesman. That's someone who speaks on behalf of the gang to the law. Then I became the gang's chief enforcer, enforcing all the punishments. That was a crazy job. I hate even thinking about the things we did. But then I became a general, overseeing all the other chiefs. When you're a general you get respect no matter where you go."

I shook my head in disbelief, because Sean no longer resembled the hateful person he described. Humility and gentleness resonated with every word.

"I had reached the pinnacle of gang life," he said. "But I was in and out of jail for stealing, attempted murder, armed robbery. While I was in jail I went to a meeting. This guy got up and shared his life, and how he found Jesus. I thought to myself, *If everything he's telling me is true then this is what I need in my life.* He didn't back off. He came to where I was standing. Tears started coming down my face. Then he gave me a Bible, which I took to my room. When I got back to my cell I put my head down 'cause I couldn't let anybody see me crying. That's when I decided my life had to change."

Tears of joy and gratitude surfaced in his eyes.

"See," he said, "I was convicted of a felony and had to go where they send the really bad guys."

"How long were you in there?" I asked.

"A year and a half. But to protect myself in prison I affiliated myself with the gang, even though I knew my days in the gang were over. But the first morning about six guys surrounded me and asked what I was all about. Instead of identifying myself as a general, I showed them my Bible. They immediately backed off.

"When I got out, I committed myself to going to church seven days a week for two and a half years straight. I didn't miss a day. I met Pastor Jones and I shared with him all I'd been through. He was open to me. The church got behind me to go to college: Got me funding and really worked with me. So now I'm back to the streets and public schools I once terrorized—but I tell kids what gangs and drugs will do to them. I tell them that a lot of my old friends and gang members are dead and others are in jail facing life. I tell them their lives can be different—if they make the right choices and hang with the right people. That's what God did for me."

Sean glanced at his pastor as if to say God had led him to the "right" person. Pastor Jones smiled knowingly, as if thanking God for leading a farm boy to the city to help people like Sean turn their lives around.

After bidding farewell to Pastor Jones and Sean, I began the return trip across town to a center for sexually abused children. I passed the schoolyard with white kids and the old man without shoes. A strange feeling rose in me as I pondered the slogan, "America, the land of equal opportunity." I wanted to believe racism and discrimination had long died, but I had to admit their embers were still burning.

God created all people equal, I said silently, *but not all people have equal chances to make something out of their lives. Millions of children—because of their race or economic status—are forced to fight for opportunities that most middle-class kids take for granted. Because of the downtrodden communities in which they live—and the frayed families that own them—each day is a fight for survival. While children like mine worry about their weekly spelling test, these kids face a constant threat on their lives.*

A blaring siren interrupted my thoughts and I noticed a drastic change in the personality of the streets. I spotted a cluster of prostitutes stationed between a pair of liquor stores. A girl—perhaps 15 or 16—wheeled a baby stroller down the sidewalk. *She should be in high school cheerleading and dating the boy next door,* I said to myself. But instead her dreams were swallowed up by one evening of pleasure. The boy next door probably got her pregnant and she was forced to substitute her pom-poms for bottles of baby formula.

The truth was I didn't know the girl's story. But I knew there were countless youths in neighborhoods like this one who felt trapped in a world they couldn't control. Some social commentators wanted us to believe all youths could achieve the American dream if they just worked hard enough and believed in themselves. But, at best, that was only a partial truth: No one could deny that neighborhoods filled with crime and poverty had nipped away at a generation's self-esteem and stolen opportunities and dreams for a brighter future. Sean was just one example of a kid turned bad by his surroundings and upbringing.

I was beginning to see that poverty and racism often went hand-in-hand. And I recognized discrimination for what it was: an assault on God's creation, and an attack on His plan for equal opportunity. *On this issue,* I said to myself, *believers don't have the option of being neutral. As followers of Jesus Christ, we have a duty to work for equal opportunity—especially for those who need a break. For Christians, this isn't a political or social issue; it's a spiritual matter we can't ignore.*

A sad reality collided in my mind as my car approached the children's center: By not speaking out more forcefully against discrimination and injustice, Christians like me had in essence accommodated hate and division in our nation.

Jesus, on the other hand, denounced bigotry and exploitation, rebuking those who fostered elitism of any kind. His friends weren't chosen based on ethnic origin or social class. Instead He gave opportunity to the poor, the suffering, and the forsaken. He touched lepers, conversed with Samaritans, freed the adulteress, befriended thieves and offered hope to the blind man. He treated everyone with dignity.

Turning off the ignition, I announced to myself, I've never mistreated people based on race, gender or economic status. But I have to admit I've lived with my eyes closed, pretending that racial issues and legislation to help the underprivileged were none of my business. Perhaps that isn't prejudice in the strictest sense, but I can't erase the thought that lives and cities are unraveling because of the apathy and silence of believers like me.

The center's receptionist ushered me into the director's humble office. Jerry was a former college athlete who saw a need among abused and forgotten kids and decided to do something about it.

Together we walked down a long hallway, where he introduced me to one co-worker after another.

"All these kids," he explained, "have been rescued from abusive situations and placed here. We do our best to make it like a home, but it's not a substitute for a home with responsible parents—if you know what I mean?"

"I understand," I said.

We entered a room crammed with bunk beds. Some of the children were already under the covers; others were in an adjacent room, their eyes fixed on a television screen.

"A lot of the kids who live here have mothers who are hookers, and their heads get messed up because they've seen them having sex," Jerry said. "You wouldn't believe what some parents do to their kids."

For several minutes the director shared one sick tale after another about the kids who resided at the center. I could tell he wasn't trying to shock or disgust me; he was trying to drive home his point: "Every day children are being victimized in America and most people don't want to hear about it; they prefer that it be buried and treated like some dark national secret.

"There are many times I look into their eyes and I can see their pain," he said. "You know, all I can really do is tell them I love them and let them know they're valuable. And, just be there for them when they need to talk."

"How do you deal with the anger?" I asked. "I mean, as far as I'm concerned, the parents should be in prison—or something worse."

"It's not my job to punish abusive parents—as much as I'd like to," Jerry said. "That's up to the courts and prison system. My job is to do everything I can to salvage these kids."

I admired how Jerry allowed the kids to cry on his broad shoulders. He recognized that each life had innate value—including children who were discarded by parents that didn't love them. There was a lot that Christians like me could learn from a social worker like Jerry.

"Why do you work here?" I asked.

"Someone has to—otherwise these kids have no chance of making it. See that boy over there?"

He pointed to a nice looking kid sitting by himself, staring at the wall in the corner of the room.

"What's his story?" I asked.

"He's 9 years old. He was abused every way you can imagine. Beaten by his father, sexually abused by his mother. When he first came here he was so disturbed we couldn't separate him from his doll."

"It's tragic," I whispered.

"You see that girl on the couch?"

I nodded.

"She was sent here because her parents abandoned her. Think about that—growing up knowing your parents didn't want you."

As Jerry continued his horrifying profiles of the kids placed in the center's care, I turned my head so he couldn't see my clenched teeth and the painful expression that had seized control of my face.

"I hate it," I snapped. "What happens to the kids when they leave here?"

"They try to find homes for most of them. But the abuse they've endured often affects them the rest of their lives. Let's just say that history often repeats itself."

I followed Jerry back through the maze of bunk beds, down the hallway to his office. Laughter and rambunctious behavior were eerily absent at the center, but Jerry possessed the ability to bring a smile to the kids' faces. They fed off of his love and attention. He had become their father figure, counselor and comforter.

Jerry's name would never be mentioned alongside Mother Teresa's, but to me he was just as much a savior. He was doing everything he could to restore hope and dignity to these little victims.

Leaving the center, a bittersweet taste rose in my mouth.

Although I was thankful these kids were receiving food, clothing and shelter, I was distressed that they weren't learning about Jesus. His name was nowhere to be found in this government-run facility. There were no Sunday School classes or believers on hand to teach them about the One who could heal their emotional scars and give them eternal life in a much better place.

I couldn't understand how God could allow the lives of these children to be destroyed.

"God, if I had just known—if other believers had known what was happening to these kids—we could have done something to protect them and show them love," I said in a sober tone.

But as soon as the words were spoken, I knew it wasn't true. I was playing mind games, trying to justify my apathy and ignorance. For the most part, Christians like me were too preoccupied with our own pursuits to follow in Jerry's footsteps. We pitied these children, but we weren't ready to make the sacrifices necessary to rescue them and teach them about Jesus.

Shame rushed in. Again and again I told God I was sorry for launching the blame skyward. He longed to help these kids more than I did. I knew that. But He was waiting for people like me to simply raise their hands and volunteer to get involved.

Before shame could flow into discouragement, I turned my attention to Washington, D.C., the next stop on my journey. I didn't know whom I'd encounter and what dangers I'd face. I just knew I couldn't bear to see any more victimized children. I was already teetering on unholy anger and feeling the urge to make someone pay for what they had done to these defenseless kids.

"If a man shuts his ears to the cry of the poor, he too will cry out and not be answered."

—Proverbs 21:13

Washing

ton D.C.

ChaPter TWelve

The Forgotten

The waters of the Potomac River rolled underneath the bridge as I entered the nation's capital. In the distance the Washington Monument pierced the low-hanging, damp air, and undulating greenbelts took on the appearance of expansive velvet carpet. Washington, D.C., was in full swing, as if expending all its remaining energies before settling in for winter.

On street corners vendors sold hot dogs and patriotic souvenirs. Students with backpacks exited afternoon buses. Business executives raced to the Metro to make their next appointment. And homeless men and women took advantage of the sun by begging for quarters.

On Pennsylvania Avenue a multitude of street people—who looked like unwilling participants in a poverty parade— caught my eye. Some hauled trash bags full of soda cans, others slept on benches, while a few simply watched the world go by. At a stoplight I was suddenly face-to-face with one of these nameless people. He knocked on my side window. As I began to roll it down my mind raced: Did he plan on robbing me? In an attempt to pretend he didn't exist I stared straight ahead.

When the light turned green I sped away.

For several blocks shame followed me like a stalker until I reached the homeless shelter I had come to tour. Hadn't I learned anything on this multi-city journey? I asked myself. Hadn't I changed?

I parked my car on a side street, and made my way to the entrance. I sneaked one last glance at the car, to ensure it was legally parked, when I spotted an unprovoked teenager spit on my windshield.

Before I could yell at him, he pivoted and our eyes met.

I shot him a stern look.

He peered back as if to ask, "What are you going to do about it?"

Nothing. Absolutely nothing. I shook my head and entered the shelter, though wondering if I was being paid back for ditching the homeless man at the intersection.

The concrete building hummed with activity. Several men, apparently pitching in, hauled boxes in and out of the place and another swept the tiled lobby.

Immediately I noticed a brass plaque on a wall: "Next time you see someone out on the street, don't pass him or her by. Ask how they're doing, say hello, and maybe even get them something to eat. Most of all tell them you care."

Again my conscience ached.

In the shelter's kitchen, which was cluttered with steel pots and pans, I met Carol, who was fast at work chopping mounds of celery, onions, potatoes and carrots.

"Preparing the soup for our guests," she explained. "Can you give me a minute?"

"No problem," I said.

She eventually handed her job off to another volunteer and launched into the tour, to help me gather research for a magazine article.

"Been in a homeless shelter before?" she asked.

"Yes, but nothing this large."

The rooms were wall-to-wall beds. The living quarters were more like a dormitory, with small bathrooms serving an entire wing of guests.

"How long have you been working here?" I asked.

"A long time."

"Why'd you choose this kind of work?"

"I guess I didn't want to be one of those people who see others suffering and do nothing about it. There won't be any excuses come Judgment Day. Jesus will say, 'Whatever you've not done for the least these, you've not done for me.'"

"Are you a Christian?" I asked, noting her reference to Matthew 25.

She paused. "Well, let's just say I admire the way Jesus lived His life."

Carol, who I assumed was in her mid-40s, led me to a room where a meeting was in progress. About 12 homeless men were seated on folding chairs in a circle. Carol excused herself momentarily, so I stood alone in the corner and listened to their conversation.

"So, how we gonna get more soap?" one man asked. "We're out of money for the month."

They fidgeted in their chairs and the leader rubbed his face before one of the men piped in. "What about collectin' cans and bottles?"

"Let's just ask for it on the streets," another resident said.

"I found some basketball shoes that are worth somethin'," a younger man added.

Carol slid back into the room and, without a word, motioned for me to follow. I wanted to linger behind to see how their soap problem was resolved, but instead, out in the hallway, I handed Carol a donation to help them out. I had to admit it made me feel a little better about myself after deserting the homeless man an hour earlier.

Carol and I proceeded to the infirmary.

"I assume some people are pretty sick when they get here," I said, noticing a man coughing uncontrollably on a bed.

"Yeah, some have been in the streets so long that they're bad off. Some of the older ones have been known to freeze to death come winter. But if people need more care than we can provide, we get them to a hospital."

"I'm curious—what happens to the bodies of the homeless when they die? Who claims the bodies?" I asked.

"Well, we do our best to claim them when we hear about

it and give them some kind of remembrance or tribute. Otherwise they're buried as John or Jane Doe—and no one ever notices they're gone. That shouldn't be—every human being has more value than that."

I wanted to say "Amen" but words failed me—perhaps because I knew it would come out sounding hypocritical or insincere. Although there were no nameless people in heaven, there were plenty of them in my world. Before embarking on this journey, I had never talked to a homeless person, let alone asked for a name.

Returning to my car, I felt convicted for my years of self-centeredness and virtual seclusion. For too many years I had lived by the adage "I'll help the poor when I feel led to." But it was becoming clear to me that Jesus rejected that philosophy.

He said when you see someone who is hungry, do whatever you can to help the person. Our first inclination must be to help—not walk away, I said to myself. *Jesus took pleasure in meeting the needs of people. If they were hungry, He wanted to give them food; if they were lonely, He wanted to be their friend; if their bodies weren't whole, He wanted to bring them healing. Jesus understood their plight because at times He was hungry, and therefore He could empathize with the starving. At times He had no place to lay His head, and therefore He could empathize with the homeless. At times He experienced pain, and therefore He could empathize with the sick and suffering. Jesus did not see the poor as freeloaders, failures or outcasts,* I continued. *He saw them as God's precious children that He needed to reach through His message of hope. He had the power to love them because He looked past their filthy exterior and saw the potential of their hearts.*

A few blocks away, I caught a glimpse of the majestic Capitol Building, whose halls echo with the footsteps of nobility. Then I passed the Supreme Court, which boasts magnificent pillars and Vermont marble steps. But, amid the grandeur of D.C., I couldn't help but sense a pervasive, unspoken arrogance that violated the spirit of "In God We Trust." At one time these buildings represented a humble reliance on God. But now, homeless men and women plodded around them day and night, perhaps symbolizing a nation preoccupied with the wrong things.

Why haven't I given more of my time to helping the poor? I asked myself. *Perhaps I bought into the false notion that all of them are victims of their own choices and therefore none of my concern. Or, maybe I've been satisfied with Sunday morning religion and have lost sight of what Christ requires of me.*

The purr of the car's engine couldn't drown out my abrupt and unrehearsed prayer: "God, I don't know what I can do to help the poor, but I'm willing. Make me more like Carol. Soften my heart and show me how to be a channel of Your blessing to hungry and thirsty people."

At the time I had no way of knowing what I was praying for. I just knew God needed to change my heart and shift my priorities so He could use my life to rescue men, women and children from the jaws of hopelessness and poverty.

ChaPter THirteen

Ella's Home

Marching up the crumbling steps to Ella's old two-story house, I spied a suspicious neighbor watching me through parted curtains.

Ella was as much a legend in the neighborhood as John F. Kennedy or Martin Luther King. She had opened her home years ago to young unwed mothers and had helped many of them flourish in life.

I pushed the doorbell but no one answered. While waiting, I read a telling sign on the porch—"A place for help."

Determining that the doorbell wasn't working, I resorted to three firm knocks. Immediately I heard shuffling feet.

The door swung open and an elderly black woman greeted me with a generous smile.

"Hello, are you the one who called?" she asked.

"Yes. As I mentioned on the phone, I'm working on a magazine article and it was recommended that I get your story."

"I really haven't been one to look for publicity," she said.

"We'll change your name in the article if you'd like. We

really just want people to know that there are people like you who sacrifice so much to help others. All I need is 30 minutes."

She nodded. "All right. Would you like a cup of coffee before we start?"

"No, thank you," I said, retrieving my tape recorder from my pocket.

Ella's home was sparsely furnished. The walls contained several plaques and crayon drawings in uneven frames. The couch felt more like a beanbag and the other furniture resembled items from a yard sale.

"Are you sure you don't want some coffee?" she asked.

"If you're going to have some, I'll have some too," I responded, deciding that it might help her relax during the interview.

A few minutes later she reentered the room with a tray and two chipped mugs. A pregnant, blonde-haired girl trailed Ella with a plate of crackers.

"When is your baby due?" I asked the girl.

"Five and a half weeks."

"Is it a boy or girl—do you know?"

She smiled and shook her head. "No, I'm waiting to find out."

Ella didn't feel comfortable sharing details of the girl's story, but just the same I felt warm inside knowing she and her baby were in Ella's care.

Ella had come to D.C. years earlier. An illness forced her into the hospital for two months, which exhausted all her money. For a short time she was homeless, before finally landing a position as a hotel dishwasher. She eventually found a government job and enrolled in university-level courses.

Some years passed and Ella squirreled away enough money to buy this house. She then worked with various social agencies to place young women in the home.

"How many girls live here?" I asked.

"Usually four or five at a time," she said.

"There aren't a lot of people who would bring girls into their home like this," I said.

She smiled. "I guess some of us just get elected to do this sort of thing."

"The world would be a better place," I said, "if there were more Ellas to go around. You're a remarkable woman."

"I'm just doing what I can. My father used to say, 'Ella, don't let the devil ride, 'cause eventually he'll want to drive.' That's what's happened in some of our cities—the devil has just about taken over. So I gotta do what I can to help fight that."

Taking off my reporter's hat momentarily, I said, "Ella, I'm going to be praying for you." She had a Crucifix on the wall so I assumed my offer wouldn't offend her.

"And please pray for my girls and their babies," she replied. "They need the good Lord's help. It's not easy for them once they're out on their own."

"I'll do that, Ella."

"Young man, can I ask you a question?"

"Sure," I replied.

"As you travel across the country, are you findin' that people are trying to help one another again?"

"Some—but, as you know, there are a lot of families out there with needs. It's overwhelming. I think a lot of people want to do something to help, but they don't know what to do."

"That's very true," she said.

"I'm curious, Ella, how do you keep from getting overwhelmed when so many people need your help?"

Her eyes closed momentarily as if considering her answer. "I learned a long time ago that I couldn't change the world. But maybe I could help change the future for a few young ladies and their babies. That's all the good Lord has asked me to do."

Ella didn't know it, but she had just preached me a sermon I needed to hear. Like a knot unraveling in my stomach, I felt a sudden sense of relief.

God doesn't expect me to do everything, but He wants me to do something, I said to myself. *It's my job to stay close to Him; it's His job to guide me to the people who need help*

*and to show me what to do. He simply wants me to remain
ready and willing.*

Pastor Bob and his wife, Sharon, had earned a strong
reputation in Anacostia, a section of D.C. They had devoted
more than 30 years of their lives to pastoring a congregation
and reaching out to children and families in southeast D.C.
I wanted to learn more about their afterschool tutoring
program and their camps for inner-city kids, so I paid them a
visit.

We rendezvoused in a room filled with a dozen children
seated at computer stations. Sharon and her son and
daughter were on hand to look over the kids' shoulders, to
tutor them on everything from math to English.

On the wall were the names of students and a chart of their
achievements.

Patting a small girl on the back, Sharon said, "This is one
of our students, and she is progressing so well."

The girl's face lit up.

"If she wants to … one day she's going to graduate from
college and do something great with her life."

Bob leaned against the door like a proud husband and
father. He could have chosen to pastor a larger church and
bask in the comforts of the suburbs. Instead his entire family
had committed their lives to the people of this depressed
area, so children like the ones in this lab could have a chance
at a better life. It was quickly apparent that Bob and Sharon
weren't chasing glory or pursuing personal objectives; they

were building a legacy of faithfulness and obedience to God.

"This is awesome," I said. "Thanks to your work, these kids are going to reach their potential and learn skills that will help them make it in the real world."

"God loves these kids," Bob said, deflecting the praise. "But, to tell you the truth, we could help so many more kids and teenagers if we just had the resources."

I kept my thoughts to myself, but I couldn't help but weigh how much of my own money—and God's—had been wasted on frivolous pursuits when servants like Bob, Sharon and Ella needed the funds to expand their work and help more people.

Not everyone has been called to work in the inner city or to journey to remote places around the world, I said silently, *but we can invest in people and outreaches that are already there. How many times has God nudged us to give generously to works like these, but we turn a deaf ear because our possessions possess us? We gauge God's blessing on how much we consume rather than by how much we share. We measure success by our earthly stuff rather than the treasures we store up in heaven.*

My thoughts drifted to my deceased father who was notorious for giving the shirt off his back to the poor. I remembered coming home from school one day and hoping to take a nap in our brand-new recliner. But, when I arrived, the chair wasn't there. My dad had given it away to someone in need. I asked, "Dad, why'd you give it away? Now we don't have one."

He replied, "Life isn't about what you can get; it's about

what you can give away."

Bob and Sharon invited me to join them for a meal in their modest Anacostia home. They knew the bane of crime, poverty and drugs, yet I marveled at how they preferred to accentuate the positive and highlight the work of God in the community. Throughout the evening, I listened to them unfold one story after another of youths delivered from drugs, families reunited and children excelling in school. They weren't ignoring the desperate needs of their community. They were simply focusing all their energies and resources on meeting needs, spreading Christ's love and giving children an opportunity to make something out of their lives. Like Ella, they were fully committed to doing everything God had elected them to do.

Ken and I made our way to the Lincoln Memorial at 11 p.m. The statue of Abraham Lincoln stared past columns at a world different than the one he fought for. His gnarled hands hung over the arms of his chair as spotlights targeted his face.

He seemed to be looking mournfully on two homeless men who had hunkered down on the marble steps, but were quickly shooed away by authorities.

At midnight when members of Congress and lobbyists were out socializing or comfortably tucked in for the night, Washington was catching its second wind. Taxis knifed through wide boulevards. Night owls ascended monuments. Trendy couples stumbled out of nightclubs.

We ventured into a park dotted with homeless men and

women. City lamps lit the park, but the area seemed dark and haunting as I passed a row of sagging cardboard huts. My eyes fell on a child who was nestled against her mother in a tattered sleeping bag. At that moment all the architectural feats and political pageantry of the city seemed insignificant.

An elderly woman seated on a bench stared at us as if we were aliens. Her frame was so mummified by layers of clothing that she resembled a tackling dummy used in football drills. Her tennis shoes didn't match, and strands of gray hair sneaked out from beneath her stocking cap.

"What's your name?" I asked softly.

The woman peered away in trepidation.

"I won't harm you," I said.

Refusing to look me in the eyes, she said, "Martha." Her voice was raspy and thick with infection.

"How long have you been living in the streets?"

"I don't live in the streets," she snapped, pointing to a sheet of plastic and a blanket strung between two trees like a pup tent.

"Do you have family?"

Martha didn't answer as she hastily picked up a brown paper bag and lumbered away.

Amid the trees were more homeless men and women, some sleeping, while others mumbled to themselves. One man warned me away from his park bench, insisting I was invading his private space.

Walking toward a tall building in the distance, I was startled by two rats the size of cats. They crossed the street and disappeared into the sewer.

"They're a problem; they carry disease," said a man perched on a bench. He wore faded green jeans and a blue sweatshirt splattered with white paint. "Do they have rabies—do you know?"

"I'm not sure, but I wouldn't take any chances," I said.

Nearby several men who were camped out in the bushes glared at us. It was strange seeing these men in their condition, and knowing the White House stood in all its glory only blocks away.

"How you guys doin' tonight? Stayin' warm?" I asked.

"Yeah—what's your name?" one asked.

"Hal and Ken—what's yours?"

"Frank."

"Are you from D.C.?" I asked.

"I've only been in this [expletive] park for a few weeks," he said. "Before that I stayed in North Carolina."

"I didn't think they'd let people sleep here."

"You can't," he said. "Those [expletive] will come by in a few hours to get us on our way. They want us in the shelters. Hey, you got a few bucks? I don't need much—just enough to get by. It's hard to find work out here when you don't have skills."

I tried to read his eyes to determine if I was being played. I reached for my wallet and gave him $10."

"So, how you gonna get off the streets?" I asked.

"Somethin' is bound to happen," he said. "Hopefully soon 'cause it's gettin' [expletive] cold out here."

"Do you believe God can help you?"

His head bobbed and he looked away. "Yeah, I believe," he said, "but God's gonna have to work somethin' out for old Frank 'cause I'm 'bout to give up."

I didn't know exactly what he meant by "giving up," but I said, "Hang in there—you're going to make it."

Moments later, he stretched out on a bench and covered his face with a newspaper. "I've got to get to sleep before they come and make me move," he said from under the paper.

Ken struck up a conversation with another homeless man, while I pressed on alone deeper into the park. It was a beautiful night for a walk and a better night for those who slept under the stars. Like a massive nightlight, the moon hid behind tall trees whose limbs bent slightly in the breeze.

I came upon an elderly woman who wore a sock on one hand. On the other, thick black dirt had settled under her fingernails. Her hair was twisted and gray and lay on the shoulders of her soiled jacket.

"Do you live out here?" I asked.

"Of course."

Catherine acted a tad crazy but her stories were tragic and heartwrenching. After she was raped, she said, her life fell into a tailspin.

"I started drinking and my family wanted nothing to do with me. So I ended up in the streets."

"That's rough," I said.

"Have you ever noticed the woman on top of the Capitol?" she asked rather oddly. "Well, you know she's facing east toward England. Maybe she's saying, 'Take that, England—America is strong despite your attempts to rule us.'"

"I never thought about that," I replied.

"Well, that's how I feel," she said. "I sit here in this park and I look south where my family lives and I say, 'Take that, I can make it without you.' But now I have all these guys out here who need me. They call me 'Mama.' I watch out for them and give them the love only a mother can give. They're my family."

"Where does your family live? Do you have children?"

A terrified look captured her face. And she promptly waved me away, forcing an abrupt ending to our conversation.

"I'm sorry, I didn't mean to upset you," I said.

She kept her head down and waved me away again.

I wandered over to the Vietnam Memorial, hoping to get

alone with my thoughts. There, leaning against the marble facade that contained the names of soldiers lost in battle, was a man dressed in patched jeans and an army-fatigue jacket.

He wiped tears from his eyes when he heard my footsteps approaching.

I walked past him reverently; then wheeled around, saying, "Are you okay?"

He lowered his head. "Yeah—okay."

"You a veteran?"

He nodded. "Yeah, lost a lot of buddies over there."

"How long were you in 'Nam?"

"About a year. Worst [expletive] year of my life."

"Do you live in D.C.?"

"No, I'm from somewhere else. I caught a ride to see the names of my buddies."

"What kind of work you in?"

"Right now I'm not. Times are tough, you know?"

"I'm trackin' with that," I said.

I could smell liquor on his breath and wondered if alcohol had followed him like an unwanted friend for the last 30 years.

"What you out here for?" he asked, turning the tables on me.

"I'm a reporter—interviewing some of the homeless."

Instantly he stood straighter.

"You're a reporter? For who?"

"I'm writing for several publications."

Anger rose in his voice. "Well, you can quote me on this: War is [expletive]. It ruined my [expletive] life. I love my country, but I don't give a [expletive] about fightin' for some other country."

"What's your name?" I asked, trying to calm him down.

"Ralph."

"Ralph, I want you to know something. I believe Jesus sent me here to talk to you tonight. He wants to be your friend. He wants to restore what you've lost."

"I thought you were some kind of reporter. You sound more like a television preacher."

"Well, let's put it this way, tonight I'm a reporter delivering a message to you. Jesus is what you're looking for."

The spotlights from the Memorial half-lit his face. Tears surfaced in his eyes, his emotions broke, and he couldn't reply. Again he covered his face with his hand.

Taking a risk, I asked, "Can I pray for you?"

He nodded—still choked up.

"Dear Jesus, be with my friend, Ralph. Let him know that You love him and You want to take care of him. Help him get a job. Help him deal with his memories of the war. And help him know that people like me look up to him."

Then I asked if he wanted to receive Jesus as his personal Savior, but he declined. "I can't do that now; I have too many issues," he said.

"Jesus knows you better than you know yourself. He knows the issues you're talking about. He wants you to talk to Him, man."

"I'll think about it," he said.

I wrote my name and contact information on a piece of paper and slipped it in his hand.

"Here's how to reach me if you want to talk sometime. Or, go to a church that teaches the Bible and talk to the pastor."

Again he dipped his head, as if contemplating my words. Then he stuck out his hand.

"Thanks for stoppin' and talkin' to me," he said in a weakened voice.

"It's my honor. Thanks for all you and your friends have done for America," I replied. "We're indebted to you."

When I walked away, I noticed him wipe more tears from his eyes, go limp, and lean back against the Memorial.

Early the next morning I interviewed a drug enforcement officer with a menacing physique. No doubt he could deliver a knockout punch if provoked by drug dealers. His affection for D.C ran deep: he had spent his adult life chasing drug offenders who threatened to tear down his city.

"Today you have a much more violent type of criminal who is not bonded to other human beings," he said. "The average criminal is more sociopathic than before. There is an utter lack of concern for other individuals. We see guys all the time who would just as soon take your life as look at you."

He stepped over to a large window and gazed out on the city landscape. "I'm also concerned about our children in cities across the country, where molestation cases are on the rise."

"What do you think is at the root of society's ills?" I asked.

He spun around as if he knew the question was coming.

"Greed," he replied.

"Not drugs?" I pressed.

"Drugs are a symptom—and not just an inner-city problem," he said. "They've taken root in the suburbs, in the business district, in our schools—they're everywhere. But why do people make, use and distribute drugs? Because they want to satisfy themselves. It's all about greed and pleasure. It's a dark world out there."

"What's the solution?" I asked, fully expecting him to launch into another theoretical speech.

His eyes flared. "The solution?" he said, pausing. "The solution is for every person to get their heads out of the sand and do their part."

Minutes before boarding a flight to Atlanta, I replayed the officer's comments in my mind. Many Christians like me had put their heads in the sand. *Sitting in front of our television sets night after night,* I said to myself, *we curse the darkness but don't do our part to bring light and hope to these dark places. On the other hand, many believers—through their actions and prayers—are brilliant lights that can't be ignored. God, I want to be that kind of Christian—one that goes beyond words and makes a real difference in the lives of people in need.*

As the flight crew made its way down the gateway, and passengers began inching toward the door, I sat motionless with my eyes closed. The smell of poverty lingered in my nose, hollow voices rang in my ears, and the sight of weary eyes passed before me like mists in an all-too-real dream.

God, I prayed silently, *what can I do to give people like Catherine and Martha an opportunity to leave their park-bench beds, cardboard huts and back-alley pads and one day walk on streets of gold? Please show me what to do.*

At that moment, like a wool blanket, a warm assurance fell on my shoulders. Somehow I knew an answer to my nagging question was on its way.

"I [Jesus] am the light of the world. Whoever follows me will never walk in darkness, but will have the light of life."

—*John 8:12*

ChaPter FOurteen

The Singer

Black Ruby was her stage name. And the streets of Atlanta were her theater. She was 23 and her eyes were brown, bright and pretty like her copper skin. She had thick lips smothered with glossy lipstick that covered her perfectly straight teeth. One tooth was gold-plated—a gift from her pimp. She wore knee-high leather boots, a black miniskirt and a seductive smile.

"Hi there," she said with a dose of southern charm that no doubt had snared many men. "You want a good time?"

"I'm not looking for a date," I said. "But I am looking for someone to talk to."

It was well past midnight. The boulevard was busy despite being part of an anemic portion of Atlanta's business district. Teens drank beer in dark parking lots as homeless men huddled in doorways arguing over who would sleep where. And, like sentries, prostitutes were planted on every corner.

This was not the city I had seen earlier in the day. Many parts of Atlanta were appealing and safe. Atlanta had established itself as a world hub for business and commerce. CNN and Coca-Cola were headquartered here. Skyscrapers stood watch over the gorgeous capital city like old statues of Confederate generals gazing at the horizon.

For two centuries Atlanta had been the "Gateway to the South," where mansions stood atop rolling hills and genteel manners prevailed. Now, as the home of the largest news network, Atlanta was gateway to the world. The city, as much as New York or Chicago, had become a purveyor of the American dream. But behind the façade of perfection, the foundations had begun to crack.

"We can talk," Ruby said, "or we can play."

"Just talk," I said as I found a seat on the bus bench Ruby occupied. "What are you doing out here?

"What does it look like I'm doin'?" she asked. "I'm workin'. Girl gotta make a livin'."

I began to scribble her quote in my notebook, even though I had a tape recorder running in my pocket.

"You a newspaper person?" she asked.

I nodded.

"Believe what you want but I do this—and I strip at the club—to feed my kids," she said. "You ain't from the agency? You ain't gonna try and take my kids away?"

"No—take it easy. Like I said, I'm a reporter. Let's just talk for a few minutes and I'll be out of here."

"How old are your kids?"

"Two and four," she said. "And I get on my knees every night and ask God to watch out for them."

"Do they know what you do?"

"No, they don't," she said. "Doubt I'll ever tell them about this [expletive]."

She smelled of inexpensive perfume and cigarette smoke.

"Are you married?"

"No, but I've got a business associate—"

"Your pimp?"

"He's an associate," she said peering down the street bitterly. "And, yes, he takes a lot of my money."

"Why do you stay with him?"

"He's all I got. You ask a lot of questions."

"Just one more: If you could, would you stop workin' the streets?"

"Of course," she said softly.

"Will it happen?"

She hesitated then held the question.

"Someday. Trust me, if I'm livin' for anything, I'm livin' to get out of here so my kids can be proud of their mama."

Sadness came over me as I pondered how her need for money had stolen her self-respect and placed her in harm's way.

"I gotta go," she said, disrupting my thoughts. "Things could get ugly if all we're gonna do is talk."

I wanted to give her some money for her kids—but I

couldn't bring myself to pad the pimp's pockets.

"Keep praying," I said at her back.

She didn't respond.

I felt like going after her to tell her that Jesus loved her and He wanted to help her get out of the business. I recoiled, however, when her pimp arrived and—from a distance—he flipped me off.

Steve and I drove toward the police precinct for a ride-along on the midnight shift. We passed an abandoned church, the bricks mildewing, the grass overrun by weeds, and the concrete steps crumbling toward the "condemned" sign on the front lawn. I could hear train whistles in the background, bringing to mind previous centuries, the Civil War, the expansion era, wandering hobos and men swinging pick-axes under the scorching sun. Tonight, as the train whistle cried in the distance, it felt ghostly, like the past coming to haunt the present.

An illness crept up my spine when we discovered we'd taken a wrong turn and we were lost somewhere in the recesses of Atlanta. The neighborhood we found ourselves in resembled crime-infested areas of other cities. But it was one thing to ride shotgun with the police into neighborhoods like this one, and quite another to be lost and on your own.

Before panic could set in, we sped toward a brightly lit street and eventually found our way. We passed stately colonial homes, family restaurants and modern schools before arriving at the refurbished police sub-station.

An officer at the front desk escorted us to the sergeant in command of the precinct. The sergeant had a military crew cut and a tight shirt that made him look like he'd been chiseled out of stone. He extended a formal hand to Steve and me and led us to the main hall where the next shift had assembled for their nightly meeting.

When roll was called the officers snapped to attention like fine soldiers—their toes lining up along a strip of tape on the floor. The sergeant walked along the line with a pencil that he tapped on each officer's chest as he spoke.

Five minutes later he dismissed the officers to their respective beats.

"What's the chest tap about?" I asked in the hallway.

"To make sure they have their vests and shock plates on," he said. "I was once shot during a robbery. I insist that all my officers wear them and you'll wear one too."

He issued a stiff warning to us to be alert during the ride-along, and introduced the respective officers that Steve and I would be riding with.

Mike, a veteran of the force, had hollow cheeks and a reedy voice. He came across as a die-hard family man. Every other sentence was about his wife and kids, and he seemed eager to get home after his shift rather than join some of his comrades at a local sports bar.

On a main avenue we passed a string of low-rent motels that advertised vacancies with blinking neon lights. I could see dimly lit front offices and empty swimming pools with rusty gates and locks. Shrubs grew out of control.

"Some guys coming home from work stop in there before they go back to their wives," Mike said. "It's pathetic."

Unexpectedly, he whipped the car around. "I see one of the kids from the girls home," he announced.

We pulled up alongside a young girl in blue sweatpants and a white sweatshirt walking down the sidewalk.

"Evening," he said, rolling down his window. "Where you going?"

"Girlfriend's house," she snapped, continuing to walk.

"This isn't the safest neighborhood. Would you like a ride?"

"No."

"Hey, why don't you just stop walkin'?" he said, his voice rising as the squad car came to a stop. "I want to ask you a few questions."

The girl stopped dutifully, staring straight ahead. I sensed her anger, especially since her fate for the evening was going to be determined by a beat cop.

We hopped out of the car.

"Identification?" Mike asked.

She shook her head no.

"Age—what, 16?" he said.

"Eighteen."

"I'm not sure you're telling me the truth, but why are you running from the shelter?"

"I'm not," she protested.

"You're not? Then where do you live? Where you goin'?"

"I don't have to tell you anything," she barked. He took her gently by the arm and guided her toward the backseat of the car.

"Have a seat. What did you say your name was?"

She tried to ignore him, but eventually gave in. "Shandell."

"What's your mother's name and phone number?" he asked patiently. "I think she'd want to know that her daughter was out on the avenue late at night."

"I don't live with my mother."

"That's right—you're going to a girlfriend's."

"I live with someone else," she said. "My aunt."

"Where were you coming from?"

"The [expletive] gas station."

"What were you doing there?"

"Nothin'."

"I'm taking you back to the shelter where you came from," he said.

"How d'ya know where I'm from?"

"I've seen you there. I know you're not 18 and your name ain't Shandell—it's Shanna."

"It's not …," she said firmly.

"Then what is it, and why did you lie to me?"

He walked away momentarily to give driving directions to a guy in another car … leaving me alone with Shanna.

"How long have you lived in the shelter?" I asked.

She paused a few beats before surrendering the truth. "A long time, since last February."

"How come they put you in a shelter?"

"My dad used to do things to me," she replied.

"What do you mean?"

"He'd beat the [expletive] out of me," she said. "That's why I'd rather live in the streets or with some friends."

"So you've run away before?"

"Yeah."

"Do you ever wish you could go back home?"

"Never," she said staring out the window. "I like living at the shelter—anywhere is better than home—but the people at the shelter are sayin' they might have to send me home."

Now I understood what had driven Shanna to the streets.

Mike jumped back in the car and heard me ask Shanna, "What do you want to be someday—when you get older?"

"I dunno," she said, suddenly playing dumb. "I don't have any ambition. They took that away from me along with everything else."

"So you never had any dreams?" I asked.

She searched my eyes to determine if I could be trusted. "Singin'," she said. "When I was a little girl I dreamed of bein' a singer."

"You have a good voice?"

She cracked a smile. "Yeah, my voice is good," she said.

"If you could, what would you sing?"

She didn't hesitate. "Hip hop, ballads, the kind of tunes you hear on the radio."

It was as if she had been waiting for someone to ask her that question for months—maybe even years.

"Would you like to make a CD someday?" I asked.

"Yeah—that'd be cool."

"How 'bout laying some vocals as a backup singer to get started?"

"As long as the songs are good," she said, as if negotiating a record deal.

For a few moments conversation ceased and we listened to the sounds of the motor, dispatch radio and wheels grinding against the pavement. Then, deflecting off the rear window came Shanna's voice, pure and soft.

"When someone loves you, it changes your life," she sang. "When someone loves you, time just stands still. When someone loves you, they always will."

As she sang, her dream seemed to unfold for a moment, like a prayer offered with a sincere heart. As she finished the second verse and glided through the chorus, we pulled in front of the home for girls.

"Time to go, Shanna," Mike said.

We escorted her to the front door.

"That was an amazing song," I said. "Who wrote it?"

"I just made it up," she replied, a broad smile spreading across her face.

"Girl, you have talent," I declared. "Don't let anyone take away your dream—no matter what."

With that, she disappeared inside—to what she and I both knew was a life of uncertainty.

An hour passed in the squad car when Mike pointed to a gold Mercedes with tinted windows. "There he is. We've got this [expletive]."

He radioed in the license plate, received confirmation, then called for backup.

Lights flashing, we chased the vehicle, eluding traffic and parked cars.

"What's going on?" I stammered, rocking back and forth

in the front seat.

"Drug dealer," Mike shot back. "We've been trying to nail this [expletive]."

Finally the Mercedes came to a halt.

"Stay down," Mike ordered.

I knew he wanted me to remain in the car, but when he jumped out of the vehicle my adrenaline kicked in and I hopped out too.

Mike pulled his gun and, on cue, I took a few steps back.

Fortunately more officers arrived and in no time they had the dealer spread-eagle against his car. They lifted a handgun from under the front seat and found $5,500 in his pocket.

With a sense of accomplishment, Mike transported the dealer to the detainment facility. Although the dealer's story may have been a compelling one, I didn't attempt to interview him while we hauled him in. His eyes—like shiny ball bearings—were terrifying. I didn't want him remembering my face.

When I entered the jail facility, fear squeezed my throat. I marched too closely to a holding cell and tattooed arms stretched through the bars as if to grab me. I managed to evade their grasp—but I couldn't avoid their verbal assault.

"Sweetheart, come over here," one burly "perp" called to me. The cells erupted in laughter.

I kept my eyes fixed on Mike and the handcuffed dealer he had in his clutches.

When the catcalls continued, Mike yelled, "Keep your [expletive] mouths shut."

Surprisingly most of them complied.

I waited patiently as Mike filed his paperwork. Meanwhile, from a distance, I studied the men occupying the cells. *Where have they come from and what turned them to hatred and violence?* I asked silently. I wondered if one of them had been arrested for beating and robbing the owner of a liquor store earlier that night. We had been called as backup to the scene of the crime and saw the blood coursing down the owner's face. *God, is there really any spiritual hope for these men?* I asked. *They seem so far away from You. But I guess the apostle Paul was a violent offender too and his life was transformed. If You can turn him around and use him to spread Your love, You can change these guys too.*

My mind shifted to thoughts of Sean in Chicago and the remarkable transformation that took place in his life. Just then Mike motioned that it was time for us to make our exit. But this time I wasn't taking any chances. I kept my distance from the cells and nearly ran out the front door.

The next afternoon I was introduced to Jean and her daughter at a homeless shelter. Jean's smile was pleasant, yet the wrinkles in her face hinted of an awful story. Dressed in hand-me-downs and bedroom slippers, Jean patted her hair as if trying to look her best for television cameras that weren't anywhere to be found. The fact I would listen to her story meant more to her than the few dollars I could have offered her from my wallet.

Six weeks earlier, Jean and her 9-year-old daughter, Lana, had boarded a Greyhound bus to escape memories of an abusive husband and a broken marriage. They didn't have money or a place to stay. They were simply desperate for a new beginning.

Arriving in Atlanta, Jean and Lana wandered into the shelter. The Christian directors opened their arms, providing them with food and a warm bed. There the mother and daughter also found Jesus Christ as their personal Savior.

With the help of caring believers, Jean landed a job and Lana was enrolled in school. Their dignity was restored. They were safe and content. Everything was coming together.

"Lana," I asked, "you're proud of your mother, aren't you?"

"Yes," she said with a telling grin.

"What do you want to be when you grow up?" I asked.

"I want to go to college and be a lawyer. And someday I'm gonna buy my mama an eight-room mansion with a computer set."

Lana hugged her mother's waist; Jean kissed her daughter's forehead. Their faces radiated with joy, because they had found a place of refuge and received the peace that comes from knowing Jesus. Many children in Lana's circumstances, including some I had met on this journey, were consumed by resentment and rebellion. But Lana was different. She was her mother's trophy—polite, obedient and respectful. In the wake of so much pain and uncertainty, Jean could peer into the eyes of her daughter and know that God had given her

a precious gift. She could send her little girl off to school
each morning knowing everything was going to be all right
because they were in God's care now.

While thanking God for rescuing Jean and Lana, I couldn't
help but lament the millions of people who were still running
from trouble and being preyed upon. Jean and Lana were
two of the fortunate ones. In their time of despair a Christian
had befriended them. All it took to change the course of their
lives was a friend who would meet their need and point them
to Jesus. I couldn't help but wonder if such a friend would
one day enter the lives of Ruby, Shanna and the men sharing
that jail cell. As I pondered that question and remembered
the lonely eyes of Ruby and Shanna, I asked God to help me
become more like Jesus and be a friend to sinners.

Leaving Atlanta, I was more aware than ever that a battle
between heaven and hell was being waged in the streets
of America. At stake were the lives of men, women and
children. I also knew I would never again be content to
watch the battle from the bleachers of my church or from
the comfort of my gated community. Powerless, self-serving,
play-it-safe religion was no longer an option for me. To be a
follower of Christ meant I had to put my faith into action; I
had to be on the front lines befriending people and rescuing
them for eternity.

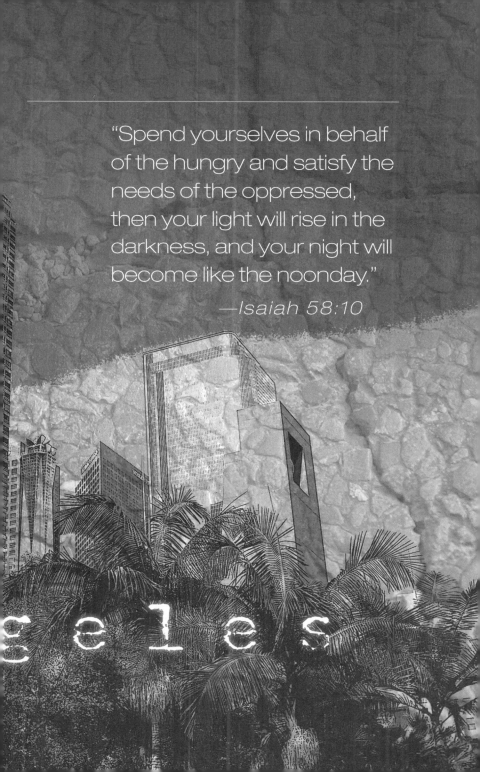

"Spend yourselves in behalf of the hungry and satisfy the needs of the oppressed, then your light will rise in the darkness, and your night will become like the noonday."

—*Isaiah 58:10*

Chapter Fifteen

Walk of Fame

I sipped raspberry ice tea in a crystal goblet while waiting for my lunch appointment at a trendy Beverly Hills café. My sunglasses deflected the Southern California rays as I waited for a budding television producer who was meeting with me as a favor to a mutual friend.

I had come to Southern California to walk the streets after midnight, to ride with the police and rub shoulders with the poor. But, along the way, I had fallen into an opportunity to hobnob with the rich and famous.

The producer, a believer, certainly didn't dust off his finest suit for our meeting. He arrived wearing jeans, a Polo and loafers. I felt out of place in my pressed dress shirt and tie. Nevertheless, I valued the chance to get an insider's view of Hollywood and to discuss how the industry had contributed to the moral crisis in our cities.

He informed me right up front that he was speaking to me off the record and his name couldn't be used in a magazine article. "I'm in Hollywood as a missionary of sorts," he said. "I don't want people in the business writing me off just because I'm a Christian."

"Are there many Christians in the industry?" I asked.

"More than you might think," the producer replied. "But this place is starved for a Christian presence. It's a huge mission field. I'm here because I believe God wants Christians to make a difference."

After sharing the details of the writing project that had brought me to Southern California, I said, "Hollywood tends to glamorize such things as gang life and prostitution, but I've seen firsthand how ugly and devastating they are."

"There's no question the wrong values are being taught," he said.

"Do the people who hold the power in Hollywood listen when Christians try to influence the themes and values in programming?"

"On occasion—but it's not just about what ends up on television or in a movie. There are people in this town who have all the money they'll ever need, but they need God just as much as a homeless person or gang member. If Christians aren't here, who's going to reach them?"

As our lunch came to an end, I began to see striking similarities between the film producer and those working for Christ in the inner city. Both had devoted their lives to reaching their respective mission fields. They shared an unusual reliance on the Holy Spirit and a fervent determination. They saw themselves as soldiers on a lifelong mission rather than tourists on a Sunday afternoon stroll. And they believed that God's power could transform any person—rich or poor.

Although his peers tended to drive European sports cars and spend weekends at the yacht club, the producer had the ability to look beyond their wealth and see their deep spiritual need. "I don't see them as millionaires," he said. "I see them as poor souls in need of a Savior."

Rising from his chair, the producer handed me his business card. "Hal, I'd appreciate it if you'd keep praying for me."

"You can count on it," I said with a handshake. "God has you here for a reason. He'll sustain you."

Ten minutes later, sitting in bumper-to-bumper freeway traffic, a simple truth raced through my mind: God has prepared every one of us to minister where He has placed us. We aren't where we are by mistake. God knows where He needs us to be a light. For some, it's at their school or workplace; for others, it's in their neighborhood or even a distant country. Some have been called to minister among the poor; and some have been called to reach out to the rich. Our duty is to simply ask God to give us our marching orders and to be willing to go wherever He leads.

Having received an invitation to a catered reception for a Hollywood premiere, I purchased a new sport coat for the occasion. My street-wear—a faded leather jacket and frayed blue jeans—didn't meet the dress code. Though this was a low-budget film, cameras flashed in frantic fashion as the lead actors emerged from their limousines. Invitees had seemingly been buffed and polished to near perfection. Hair was coiffed, skin was tan, and teeth were bleached white.

While studio elites nibbled on crackers topped with caviar and sipped champagne, I snapped up a bottle of water and found a chair off to the side of the room.

Overhearing several conversations, I quickly discovered that these gatherings were part of a networking game. Every conversation seemed to include unabashed weaseling, someone's latest achievement and some big-ticket purchase.

I set my water down and waded into the throng. A hip couple entered my path. After introducing myself, I quickly learned they had developed a pilot for a television network. "Sometime in the spring we hope to be on the air," he said.

"How do you fit into all this?" the wife asked.

When I told them I had met one of the producers, they leaned in closer as if we were old friends.

"What do you do in the business?" he asked.

"I'm not in the business," I replied.

"Oh," said the woman, obviously disappointed.

They promptly pivoted and entered another huddle—one that had clout in the industry.

As much as I wanted to chastise the couple for being shallow and superficial, I had to admit that I'd seen Christians treat people in a similar fashion. *How many times have we gravitated to those who are popular and healthy and turned away from those who are lonely and broken?* I asked myself.

My eyes scanned the room filled with Hollywood nobility and I found myself raising the same question I had posed days earlier in the Atlanta jail: *Lord, is there really any spiritual hope for these people? They are so far from You.*

Once again my hopes soared as I reflected on Christ's death on the cross and the power of His love. *Jesus gave His life for the sinners of Hollywood too,* I said to myself. *He's not impressed by their Oscars, nor dissuaded by their failures. He's seeking the soul of every man, woman and child, no matter where they live or what they do. He loves these people just as much as He loves believers. Every person is equally important to God.*

The following afternoon, I found myself sitting in the immaculate office of a motion picture executive. A friend of mine had met the woman weeks earlier and she had invited him to take a back-door tour of the massive studio. I merely tagged along.

For the next hour and a half she escorted us from one set to the next. It was like a fantasy to see actors crossing the lot and others ducking in and out of trailers. We met numerous studio personnel who shook our hands as if we were one of them.

Our host was attractive, stylish and had obviously spent a lot of money preserving her looks and refining her wardrobe. Though only 30, she had ascended rapidly in the entertainment business. A lot of that, I surmised, was due to her natural talent, but I wondered if someone with influence had helped her rise faster than most.

"So what's a typical day for you?" I asked.

As if reciting lines from a screenplay, she broke down her average day. She rose early, she said, exercised, had business meetings for breakfast, lunch and dinner. Each day she put in 10 to 12 hours at the studio. At night she unwound by shopping or clubbing with her friends.

"Are you happy with what you do for a living?" I asked.

"Sometimes," she said honestly. "But ..."

She hesitated.

"But, what?" I pressed.

"It's not without its challenges," she said. "If a film flops I'm one of the people they come gunning for. They look at the numbers, and the millions of dollars they've pumped into a film, and think the only reason it could fail is because it wasn't marketed well. That burden lies with a group of us."

"So why do you do it?"

"It pays well. You know, the car, nice house, great vacations, and the people I work with. I don't mean to be arrogant or snobby, but who wouldn't want my job?"

"But is it fulfilling?"

"Sometimes," she said.

"Do you go to church? Is that part of your routine?"

"I pray to God, but that's about it."

Our conversation continued and I sensed that although she had tasted what the world had to offer, she longed for something more. She knew something was missing in her life, but she didn't know where to find it.

Unfortunately she dashed out of the office to another

appointment before I could point her in the right direction.

Returning my visitor's badge to the front gate, I surmised that there were many in Hollywood just like her: People who were unknowingly searching for significance and purpose. Fame and fortune had failed to satisfy their empty souls—so, at night, they hop from one posh club to another, desperately looking for something to fill the void in their lives. They roam the streets of Los Angeles in chauffeured limos as aimlessly as homeless men and women push shopping carts on the sidewalks of D.C.

Exiting the studio, I fell into a silent prayer: *God, help us not to write off anyone—whether it's an actor in a guarded mansion, a prostitute in a dingy hotel, or a homeless man in a dark alley. Give us the vision to be a church without walls—one that does not give up on the millions who live in our cities nor neglects the power brokers from Pennsylvania Avenue to Hollywood Boulevard. Help us not to isolate ourselves in comfortable sanctuaries but rather to go to the lost—wherever they may be.*

That night I walked alone outside the famous Mann's Chinese Theater in downtown Hollywood. I read the names of celebrities inlaid on the stars of The Walk of Fame. I knew my name would never be alongside theirs, but that didn't matter. God knew my name and He wasn't looking for more superstars; He was looking for servants who were into obedience rather than accolades. I had always believed God had a plan for my life, but I wasn't always confident that His plan would measure up to my expectations. Now I understood that I had overrated the importance of my

vocation and achievements and underestimated simple
obedience to God—wherever that might take me.

As I walked, I prayed silently for the studio executive,
the producer, and the celebrities whose names I read on
the sidewalk. I also prayed about my own future. I didn't
know what God had in store for me, but I knew I was finally
willing to go anywhere and take on any task He had for me.
Money and prestige were no longer demands. All I asked was
that God would make me more like Christ and somehow use
my life to lift the fallen and forsaken.

Sitting alone in a restaurant at LAX—awaiting my flight
home—I stretched the *Los Angeles Times* in front of my
face like a shield. My eyes simply stared at the page because
my mind was a thousand miles away. Like a computer slide
show, the faces I'd encountered in the eight cities ran through
my mind.

*I've seen the pain of victims, peered into the eyes of evil,
and witnessed the faith of heroes—but what will it take to
bring these cities the love of Jesus?* I asked, floating between
a thought and a prayer. *These cities need to be reborn. The
decrepit buildings are the result of crumbling families and
fading hopes. If people's lives are restored, the physical
beauty of these communities will return as well. But, God,
how do we do that?*

Like an answer from heaven, Isaiah 58:10 came to my
mind: "Spend yourselves in behalf of the hungry and satisfy
the needs of the oppressed, then your light will rise in the
darkness, and your night will become like the noonday."

With the newspaper still hiding my face, I brushed tears from my eyes before they could trickle down my cheeks. This time I wasn't crying in behalf of the desperate people I'd met on my journey or agonizing over the great need in our cities. These were tears of gratitude, because I sensed God was birthing a vision in my heart to help reconnect the church to the physical and spiritual needs of desperate communities. I also sensed He was preparing an army of compassion to spend themselves in behalf of the hungry and the oppressed—to go around the world offering immediate solutions and eternal promises. With food in their hands and a message in their hearts, they would bring light where there was none. I had no doubt we were on the threshold of a global movement of compassion. I only hoped God would allow me to be a part of it.

I threw my backpack over my shoulder and headed to the gate. My eight-city tour had come to an end, but I knew my quest to become more like Christ and to make my life count was just beginning.

Hal Donaldson's personal and spiritual journey to dark places in America stirred him to action. Less than six months after he completed his inner-city tours, he loaded a pickup truck with groceries and drove to an impoverished community. There, he distributed bags of food and shared Christ's message of love and hope.

Today, that pickup has grown into a fleet of tractor-trailers and a large nonprofit organization known as Convoy of Hope. The organization has provided tangible hope to millions of people in need in the United States and around the world through food distribution, medical and dental screenings, job fairs, and much more.

Convoy of Hope has been lauded for its community-wide events, disaster response initiatives, and its ability to bring together churches, businesses, government and social agencies to transform communities with compassion.

Chapter 1   Naked in New York

1. How would you respond if you saw someone in need lying in the gutter? How would Jesus respond?

2. How would you react if a homeless person walked into your church?

3. Do you allow others' opinions to keep you from befriending or helping people who aren't popular or as well off as you?

4. Do you think God loves believers more than nonbelievers? Do you love believers more than nonbelievers?

5. What did Jesus mean by Matthew 25:34-46?

Chapter 2 The Caravan

1. Is there a difference between holiness and separation from sinners?

2. Describe some tangible ways you can reach out to people like a prostitute or a homeless man.

3. In what ways have you given up on people who don't know Jesus?

4. How do we know when to reach out and when to walk away from someone in need? Is it ever okay to ignore a person in need?

5. Have you ever acted like a Pharisee?

Chapter 3   Tears and Fears

1. When was the last time you cried for someone who didn't know Christ?

2. How long has it been since you shared your faith with a nonbeliever?

3. How many non-Christian friends do you have and what can you do to get to know more nonbelievers?

4. Before you make a purchase, do you ever stop to consider the needs of others?

5. Is there anyone beyond Christ's reach?

Chapter 4   Hookers' Hotel

1. Do Christians have a responsibility to take the gospel to dark places?

2. What does your church do to stay connected to the needs of the community?

3. What are the consequences of sin?

4. Do believers sometimes refrain from reaching out to suffering sinners because they believe they are getting what they deserve?

5. What are some ways that Satan keeps people in bondage?

Chapter 5 Guns and Thieves

1. How can we show love to those who are living in sin without being judgmental?

2. What would you do if asked to go into a crack house to share the message of Christ?

3. What does the Bible say about fear?

4. What did Jesus witness and endure 2,000 years ago that He found repulsive?

5. What can we do to prepare ourselves for uncomfortable opportunities to share Christ's love?

Chapter 6   A Child's Nightmare

1. What would you do if you became aware of a domestic violence situation and a wife or child was in danger?

2. Describe some ways Christians or churches can combat domestic violence.

3. Why doesn't God prevent harm from coming to innocent children?

4. What part does prayer play in the prevention of abuse?

5. If you could talk to abusive parents, what would you say to them?

Chapter 7   Cobain 'Lives'

1. Why do teenagers run away from home and what can be done to prevent it?

2. What impressions do nonbelievers have that keep them from going to church?

3. What would you say to teenagers who are considering running away? What would you say to a friend who was planning to run away?

4. How can you acquire the boldness and courage to share your faith in Christ?

5. How does pride hinder your evangelistic efforts?

Chapter 8   The Chase

1. Would you be afraid to rub shoulders with someone who has AIDS?

2. What can you do to show the love of Christ to those who have AIDS?

3. Would someone who has AIDS be accepted in your church?

4. How can one oppose homosexuality and, at the same time, show Christian love to homosexuals?

5. Would you treat someone differently if you found out he or she had AIDS?

Chapter 9 Killer at 16

1. Why do people join gangs?

2. What can be done to help someone get out of a gang?

3. What can you and your church do to prevent youths from turning to gangs?

4. What would you do if a runaway or gang member asked for your help?

5. Is there someone you know who faces trouble at home and needs a friend?

Chapter 10   Gangland

1. Why is crime and violence so prevalent in our society?

2. Why don't more gang members come to Christ?

3. What community programs could a church participate in to reach members of gangs?

4. What church outreaches can be established to reach out to members of gangs?

5. In what ways have Christians given up ground to the enemy?

Chapter 11   Children of Sorrow

1. In what ways do discrimination and racism show their ugly faces?

2. Have you ever seen someone subjected to racism or discrimination?

3. What can churches do to fight discrimination?

4. Do Christians have an obligation to help abused kids? If so, what should be done?

5. If an adult was abused as a child and is still suffering from its lingering effects, what can Christians do to help the person overcome the pain of his or her past?

Chapter 12 The Forgotten

1. Do our possessions and comfort keep us from empathizing with the poor and offering a helping hand?

2. What did Jesus do for the poor and suffering?

3. If you lost everything, do you think you could survive on the streets?

4. Have you ever been in a homeless shelter? If so, what did you see?

5. Because some who claim to be homeless are not really in need, does that keep you from helping any of them?

Chapter 13   Ella's Home

1. What are your first thoughts when you see an unwed teenage mother?

2. Do you sometimes become so overwhelmed with the need in the world that you throw up your hands and do nothing?

3. Are there inner-city workers and ministries that deserve your help and support?

4. Do you believe some homeless people are simply victims of misfortune and abuse? Give some examples.

5. How do Christians "put their heads in the sand" and ignore the problems of their communities?

Chapter 14   The Singer

1. Does God hear the prayers of prostitutes and drug dealers?

2. What can be done to help people who are lonely?

3. What can be done to penetrate prisons with the gospel of Jesus Christ?

4. Whom do you know whose life was turned around by an encounter with Jesus Christ?

5. Do you pray for God to put nonbelievers in your path so you can share the love of Christ with them?

Chapter 15   Walk of Fame

1. Why is it more difficult for people who are rich to serve God?

2. Does God have a specific plan for our lives? Does He care about our professions?

3. Are you living out Isaiah 58:10?

4. What can you do to break out of the religious bubble?

5. What are you going to do to reach out to more people in need?

- Deuteronomy 15:7-11
- Leviticus 19:9, 10
- Job 5:15, 16
- Psalm 14:6
- Psalm 82:3
- Psalm 140:12
- Proverbs 14:20
- Proverbs 14:31
- Proverbs 21:13
- Proverbs 31:9
- Isaiah 25:4
- Isaiah 61:1
- Amos 2:7
- Zechariah 7:8-10
- Matthew 19:21
- Luke 4:18
- Luke 14:13, 14
- Acts 9:36
- Acts 10:4
- Romans 3:23
- 2 Corinthians 8:9
- Galatians 2:10
- James 2:2-9

To know God and be ready for heaven, follow these steps:

A. Admit you are a sinner.
"There is no one righteous, not even one … for all have sinned and fall short of the glory of God."
Romans 3:10,23   (See Romans 5:8; 6:23.)

Ask God's forgiveness.
"Everyone who calls on the name of the Lord will be saved."
Romans 10:13

B. Believe in Jesus (put your trust in Him) as your only hope of salvation.
"For God so loved the world that he gave his one and only Son, that whoever believes in him shall not perish but have eternal life."
John 3:16   (See John 14:6.)

Become a child of God by receiving Christ.
"To all who received him, to those who believed in his name, he gave the right to become children of God."
John 1:12   (See Revelation 3:20.)

C. Confess that Jesus is your Lord.
"If you confess with your mouth, 'Jesus is Lord,' and believe in your heart that God raised him from the dead, you will be saved."
Romans 10:9   (See verse 10.)

Salvation Prayer

"Jesus, You died upon a cross, and rose again to save the lost. Forgive me now for all my sins. Come, be my Savior, Lord and Friend. Change my life and make it new. And, help me, Lord, to live for You." *

Signature_____

Date_____

* *Prayer written by Matt and Sherry McPherson–AutumRecords.com*

For more information about the efforts of Convoy of Hope to bring help to people in need—and to learn how to get involved—go to **www.convoyofhope.org.**

To learn how to have your own "Midnight in the City" experience, go to **www.convoyofhope.org.**

Contributions to help feed hungry children and their families can be sent to:

Convoy of Hope
330 S. Patterson Ave.
Springfield, MO 65802
417-823-8998

Hal Donaldson is national director of communications for the Assemblies of God and president of Convoy of Hope. He and his wife, Doree, reside in Springfield, Mo. They have four daughters. He is a graduate of Bethany University and San Jose State University, where he received his bachelor of arts degree in journalism-reporting/editing. He is the author of more than 20 books.

Kirk Noonan is an associate editor of Assemblies of God publications. He resides in Springfield, Mo., where he lives with his wife, Janna, and their three children. He is a graduate of Bethany University and Regent University, where he received his master of arts degree in journalism-professional writing. He is the author of *The Search*.

Other books from Onward Books:

Trusting God

A Quiet Escape

Living Like Jesus

Revival Sermons

Power for Living

The Silk Road

Living Free

Pleasing God, Pleasing You

The Vow

Woman of Courage

Parenting

Portraits of Success

For a complete list of books offered by Onward Books, Inc. and an order form, go to **www.onwardbooks.com** or write or call:

Onward Books, Inc.

4848 S. Landon Court

Springfield, MO 65810

417-890-7465